The RUNES
Workbook

D1319486

The RUNES
Workbook

A Step-by-Step Guide to Learning the Wisdom of the Staves

LEON D. WILD

METRO BOOKS
NEW YORK

This 2008 edition published by Metro Books,
by arrangement with Lansdowne Publishing Pty Ltd.

Text: Leon D. Wild
Designer: Robyn Latimer
Illustrator: Corrie Cunningham

Metro Books
122 Fifth Avenue
New York, NY 10011

ISBN-13: 978-1-4351-0814-1

Printed and bound in China.

1 3 5 7 9 10 8 6 4 2

Dedicated to my wife, Danielle Akayan.

ACKNOWLEDGMENTS
To the Yrmin Drighten, Dr Stephen Edred Flowers, who taught me to Seek the Mysteries.
Without his Work and encouragement this book would have been much harder to write.
I am also extremely grateful for his permission to use translations of the Rune Poems and
other work. And I raise a mead-horn in gratitude to those who have helped me on my way:
Dr Michael A. Aquino, Don Webb, Dan Bray (especially for help with Ásatrú practice and
pronounciations), Neville Drury, Ian Read, Peter Andersson, Eric Kauschen, Pat Hardy,
Haukur Thor Thorvardarson, Helen & Quintin Phillips, and my family—especially Sarah Wild,
Jan Davis, and Enid McIlraith. And to all of my friends in the Rune Gild.

FOREWORD

The runic quest is a great undertaking. As has become well known by now, a rune is not simply a letter of some arcane and half-forgotten northern European alphabet, but rather denotes the idea of a mystery or secret. Our ancestors clearly saw the use of symbols to communicate over time and space first and foremost as a mode of encoding meaningful messages both from and to the gods.

The runes are a gateway to a whole world of mythic symbolism that is virtually encoded in our blood, bones, and the language we speak. Clearly the English language has sounds that the Roman alphabet could not handle at the time it was adopted for writing English. This is why we now have to use two letters to represent some of our single sounds, for example, "th" and "ng." For both of these there was a single rune. This bit of esoteric information hints at the solution to a mystery, which, if you absorb the contents of this book, you will perhaps be able to discover for yourself.

Serious writing on the magical and self-developmental aspects of the Germanic runic system has now been around for little more than twenty years. The runes constitute a complete and deep-level symbology with an authentic and traditional basis. This reality has been often obscured by the writers of rune books who simply did not do their homework. In matters of esoteric knowledge, research is often not enough. The writer needs to be seasoned in his material. The tradition he delves into must have in some way become a part of him, of the very fiber of his being, before he sets out to write on the subject. Mr. Wild will not lead you astray in these matters.

A true rune book is not something to be read and put down. It is a book of secrets that must be studied over time, absorbed, and experienced. To read the runes aright requires a good deal of inner work from the reader. Here the writer has done his work; now the quest is in your hands.

EDRED THORSSON, 2003

CONTENTS

INTRODUCTION: THE JOY OF RUNES

Runes wilt thou find and rightly read,
of wondrous weight,
of mighty magic…
HÁVAMÁL

A MYSTERY OR SECRET

Runes* are the letters of a special alphabet used by the ancient peoples who spoke Germanic languages such as Scandinavian, German, Swedish, Danish, Icelandic, Norwegian, and English. The script was carved on wood, stone, or metal, and the inscriptions were often intended for magical purposes.

The rune is more than just a letter. The very word "rune"—from the Old Norse, Old English, Old High German, and Gothic—means "mystery" or "archetypal secret." If you dare to make the runes your own, you can expect to have your life taken in strange and interesting directions as you seek the mysteries and become a truer person.

The rune is a complex unit. Its form, its sound, and its number all bear symbolic meanings. This book will explore all of these levels of meaning.

THE RUNE SYSTEM

This workbook delves into the world of the Elder **Futhark**, the oldest runic system, or "alphabet." We will start by looking at this system, as the later runic systems are dependent on the **Elder** for their lore, names, and shapes.

Runes were organized in a row called the Futhark, taken from the first six **rune staves** (the stave is the name for the physical shape of the rune). In runes, these staves are written: ᚠᚢᚦᚨᚱᚲ ("th" is one rune). The naming of the rune system is similar to the way the word "alphabet" is derived—from the names for the first two letters (alpha and beta). The runes were ordered in three families called **Aetts** (eights).

*Terms described in the glossary (pages 186–187) are highlighted in **bold italic** the first time they are used.

The rune staves are angular because they were designed to be carved into wood, and it is easier to carve angular staves with a knife. Angular shapes stand out better when carved in wood, especially when carved against the grain.

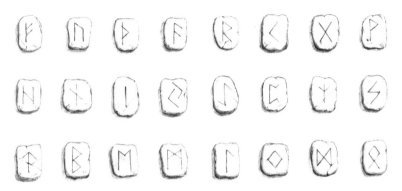

The complete Elder Futhark sequence

The Kylver Stone, in Gotland, Sweden, 350–475 c.e., has one of the earliest depictions of the complete Futhark sequence. It also has a cryptic coded sign and a magical utterance. The complete inscription is **futharkgwhnijpæzstbemlngdo** (plus cryptic sign and palindrome **"sueus"**).

SELF-KNOWLEDGE

The runes are mysteries both within us and beyond us. Though their system is an esoteric one, it is very pragmatic: the runes are ours to work with for particular self-directed ends. The runes can transform you—they can reawaken the lore of your soul in a way that is both profound and practical. They ask you to know yourself, and they provide keys to do exactly that. With the runes, you will be able to explore the mysteries of who you are and possibly work on some of the fetters that hold you back from what you need to do in order to realize your potential fully.

You will need no prior experience in any other esoteric traditions in order to work with the runes. Instead, we introduce in this workbook a number of useful mind tools to help you get the most out of learning the runes. These include:

- the keeping of a runic journal
- concentration
- visualization
- meditation

The runes offer you a chance to transform yourself and to interact with the mysterious forms encoded in them and the hidden powers of the **Nine Worlds**, in which humans interact with mythological beings and the gods (see Chapter Three). May they bring you joy, knowledge, power, and wisdom!

Reyn til Runa (Seek the Mysteries)

USING THIS WORKBOOK

This book is a workbook. It is designed to enable you to gain a basic understanding of the esoteric aspects of the runes and some of the history, mythology, and tradition behind them. It will introduce you to aspects of the tradition, provide practical exercises, and build up your knowledge of runes and how to apply them to your life.

The Runes Workbook will take a few months to complete, depending on how much time you can devote to things runic. Read through the book first and then reread carefully as you work through the exercises.

Chapter One outlines the history, mythology, literature, and magic of the rune world.

Chapter Two provides you with tools to help you begin your rune work.

Chapter Three explores in depth the mythological world of the runes: the places, the beliefs, and the beings.

Chapter Four, the central chapter, details the essential meaning of each rune, with exercises to help you understand and enact the symbolism.

Chapter Five examines runic divination and looks at using runes to answer questions, reflect on problems, and discover more about yourself.

Chapter Six focuses on magical practices using the runes.

Chapter Seven gives examples of the runes in literature and runic inscriptions.

Chapter Eight introduces you to the ethical guidelines of the Nine Noble Virtues and the Sixfold Goal, ways for rune workers to lead fulfilling lives.

A SENSE OF MYSTERY

The best attitude to approaching the runes is to cultivate a sense of mystery. Do not take them up with too many expectations—then you will find that working with them will take you on paths that are at once intensely personal and timelessly eternal. You will learn how to journey in the runic realms and follow new paths to self-transformation. This book will open up worlds of magic, myth, and mystery to you.

TOOLS FOR RUNE WORK

These items may come in handy for your rune work:
- a red pen or brush with red paint for creating runic cards
- a hobby knife for creating rune staves
- a special cup (a drinking horn if you can find one)
- a black cloth in which to wrap your runes
- a white cloth on which to cast runes
- a small supply of wood or wind-fallen branch, one inch in diameter, for making rune lots
- stiff cardboard for making rune cards
- a runic journal—a blank, red-covered journal

YOUR RUNIC JOURNAL

Keeping a runic journal will enable you to record your runic activities and help you observe your development as you learn more about the runes and uncover their mysteries.

Do the following to help maximize your rune work:
1. Before you start working through this workbook, you will be asked to write your goals in your runic journal—not just goals for your study of the runes, but also your goals for all areas of your life—education, career, love, and so on.
2. When you update your runic journal as you work through this book, write down each time:
    a) the steps you took toward attaining your goals,
    b) your most interesting thought about the runes,
    c) any plan for the immediate future to help you further your goals,
    d) any interesting coincidences that have happened in your life, and
    e) any significant dreams.
3. After you have completed each workbook exercise, write in your runic journal the date, time, your activities and practices, any impressions gained, and insights reached. This will form a valuable record of your work and, in time, give you a map of your journey, as well as hints for areas that require further work. Be honest with yourself.

Runic Journal

Workbook exercises

Date

Time

Activities and practices

Impressions gained

Insights reached

Updating my runic journal

Steps I took toward attaining my goals

My most interesting thought about the runes

Plans to further my goals

Interesting coincidences that have happened

Significant dreams

 ## WORKBOOK EXERCISES

1. In your runic journal and as quickly as you can (about two minutes), write down five goals you have for any area of your life—education, career, love, travel, etc.
2. Now, on a fresh page and taking all the time you need, compose a list of ten life goals. You may or may not, after consideration, choose to include the goals you wrote down in question 1.
3. As you begin your search into the mysteries of the runes, think about the mysteries within you. What is the lore of your own soul—the secrets and stories you hold about your ancestors, your dreams, your beliefs? Make some notes about this in your runic journal and revisit these notes later as you work through this workbook.

CHAPTER ONE

RUNES—OLD WAYS IN A NEW WORLD

Learn about the history, mythology, literature, and magic of the runes.

ORIGINS OF THE RUNES

The runes were probably in use from some time before the beginning of the common era (C.E.). The rune inscription generally agreed to be the earliest is on the Meldorf brooch from Germany, with its inscription of **ITHIH** (**IᚦIᚺ**), probably the name of a *rune master* (an expert in, and teacher of, runes).

There are various theories about the origins of the runic script. The runes may have been adapted from a culture with which the Germanic peoples were trading or they may have begun as the script of Germanic soldiers returning home after working in the Roman legions. But the runes do not match the order and form of the southern European alphabets and could well have been created by an inspired rune master or rune-working group.

FROM THE MAGICAL TO THE MUNDANE

Ancient rune inscriptions were widespread across Europe, from the cold shores of Greenland to the warm climes of the Mediterranean and deep into Russia. Wherever those skilled at runes traveled, they left a fragmented but insight-lending trail of rune inscriptions on everyday items—jewelry, weapons, amulets, and memorial stones. Runes even appeared as graffiti in days long gone.

The inscriptions vary from the magical to the mundane. A theory is that the earliest rune inscriptions were for magical and religious purposes, but later were used for ordinary reasons too. The magical inscriptions are an expression of the will of the magician carving them. These inscriptions often state the aims of the magic and in many cases intensify the will with a potent magical formula. *Bracteates* are gold, coinlike tokens with religious significance. They are often inscribed with runes and their inscriptions and images point to the cult of **Odin**, lord of the runes (see Chapter Three).

Most famous are the rune stones of Scandinavia, especially in Norway, Sweden, and Denmark. In the early inscriptions, a dual magical and religious focus is apparent. They often mention the title **Erulian**, possibly an equivalent of "rune master." Later stones were often raised in memory of lost warriors or other family members. These were not gravestones in the modern sense; many of the rune stones commemorate brave warriors lost while on their adventures or in the service of a leader.

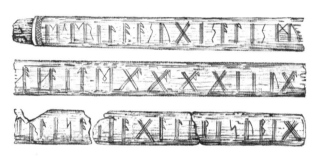

An early inscription, on wood, shows that runes were used to increase the usefulness of an object. It comes from the Kragehul spear shaft of Fyn in Denmark (300 C.E.). This inscription contains the name of the rune master and a formula for consecration. The spear was the weapon most identified with Odin, lord of the runes.

I, the Erulian Ansugislaz. I am called the High One. I give protection, I give protection, I give protection. I give very holy protection. Hail [runic magical sequence ᚠᛁᚾᛒᛁᛅ].

Ekerilazasugaisalasemuhahaiteagagagagagginuaghe ...lija...hagalawijubig

The Tryggevaelde stone in Denmark shows the magical practice of having the god Thor hallow the runes (see page 24).

CARVINGS ON WOOD AND STONE

The carvings on the rune stones were made with a type of pick hammer and must have required significant effort to carve and erect. The stones were often colored—red was sometimes used for the lettering, symbolic of the blood that animates living creatures.

Runes were also carved onto mobile objects, such as wooden staves, weapons (notably spears, swords, and axes), brooches, rings, and household objects such as combs. It probably took less effort to carve an inscription onto wood or scratch it into metal than to chip away with a pick hammer on a stone slab. Wood was also far easier to carry. However, many inscriptions on movable objects have probably been lost to us because of the medium they were carved on—wood, bone, and iron disintegrate much faster than stone.

OLD WAYS AND OLD GODS

The modern runic revival follows the cultural, magical, and religious belief system often described as the Old Ways, the **Troth** or **Ásatrú**. Both Ásatrú and the Troth generally refer to the same concept, which is the practice of keeping **true** to the ancestral religion of our Germanic ancestors. It is a holistic approach to life, magic, and the worlds of both ourselves and the gods.

This book introduces a number of figures and concepts in the Troth worldview, such as the cosmology, beings, and role models. Practicing rune work enables you to gain a deeper insight into the world of the Troth, which you can carry further once you have worked through this book. See Resources, pages 184–185, for further references you can use to help you keep true.

The myths of the old Germanic gods are inscribed in runic lore, and learning about them as a beginner rune worker will enrich your experience and provide a much deeper approach for your understanding of the runes and of your life beyond them (see Chapter Three).

THE RUNE GILD

The **Rune Gild** is a specialized group dedicated to the god Odin. It sees itself as the rebirth of the Elder Gilds of rune masters in northern Europe. A gild in medieval times was known to offer specialized training and support, protection, and friendship for those who had a particular skill or craft. The modern group has its roots in both academia and early Ásatrú groups in the United States and England. The Rune Gild works with runes in all of their applications, such as divination, rune magic, meditation, rune yoga, and the general perspective that comes from the **Odian** path (one who emulates, rather than worships, Odin).

DIVINATION

Divination using the runes will help you to know your **Wyrd** (fate). This is a specialized type of rune work, although it has been popularized so much that many think divination is the major focus of the runes. In this workbook, we outline the process of divination and try to show that it is a sacred art that should be performed only when necessary, for example, during major festivals or life events.

GALDRA: RUNE MAGIC

In this workbook you will be introduced to **Galdra**, or rune magic. "Galdra" means "to crow like a raven," and refers to the verbal aspects of the runes, such as rune names, poems, and formulas. Rune magic often has a verbal component.

Rune magic focuses on the themes of knowledge, power, and causing change in the world and the self. Magic is a transformative art that allows us to shape ourselves or the world. Like any art, it requires aptitude and practice. With dedication, the runes will help you with transformation in one form or another. Magic is the synthesis of all aspects of the runes—the history, myths, psychology, and cosmology. Learning about Galdra will help the rune worker understand the runes.

 WORKBOOK EXERCISE

List in your runic journal your goals for your study of the runes. Return to this list again as you work through this book. Reframe your goals if necessary.

THE WORLD TREE

There are Nine Worlds in the runic tradition (see Chapter Three). These worlds exist simultaneously and are multidimensional. They are connected by the **World Tree**, **Yggdrasill**. Midgard (Middle Earth) is the most important world for humans. It is where humans interact with gods and mythological beings, the place of human struggles and joys. In this book, you will learn about the structure and interactions of the worlds linked by Yggdrasill and about the cosmology of these worlds. You will also learn more about yourself and the way you relate to your world.

RUNES IN LITERARY TRADITIONS

Those who seek to reconstruct the runic tradition face many difficulties with the material. There are only about 250 inscriptions in the Elder Futhark corpus. To reconstruct a tradition from this alone would be near impossible. The reconstructive effort has been greatly assisted by nonrunic archaeological finds. These have helped piece together the social and cultural background that is necessary for understanding the runes. Major archaeological finds that have helped the reconstructive effort include the results of excavations of burial mounds, towns, halls, and even temples.

The literature that survives from the pagan Germanic tradition has also empowered the runic awakening. These works have been enjoyed and studied for hundreds of years. The literary tradition is mainly from the later runic era, although valuable evidence survives from the period of Classical Roman contact with the Germanic tribes, such as in Tacitus's *Germania*, where the ritual of rune casting is observed (see Chapter Five).

The main runic literary tradition encompasses the *Eddas*, the Sagas, and the rune poems. Also important are other manuscript-based traditions and the later magical *Galdrabóks* (spell books), written in the 1500s. Most important are the two *Eddas*, the mythological masterpieces of Iceland.

ABOUT THE EDDAS

The *Eddas* contain much of the rune lore. The Elder *Edda* is a collection of about forty poems that were compiled by an unknown Icelander in the thirteenth century; the poems had been copied from manuscripts that are now lost. It has been handed down from pagan times, although it was put into writing only after the conversion of Iceland. This *Edda* contains powerful mythological tales, all of which are essential reading for advanced rune workers. The tales include *Hávamál*, *Voluspá*, and *Sigdrífumál*.

The Younger *Edda* is a handbook of poetics on the most-loved Northern mythological themes, written c. 1220 C.E. by Snorri Sturluson, a major figure in the Icelandic literary tradition. Sturluson was a Christian, but his poetry was Icelandic first—and hence a mixture of the **heathen** and the secular. He wanted to educate the next generation of Icelandic poets about the pagan poetry traditions so that they could live on, as they were in danger of becoming lost as a result of the cultural changes occurring in Iceland.

The *Edda* tradition would not have survived had it not been for the cultural and geographic isolation of Iceland. This country was founded around 870 C.E. by Norwegians seeking their autonomy from King Harald Fairhair, who wished to impose his rule and taxes on all of Norway. Iceland was renowned for its literary skill, and its **skalds**, or poets, were in high demand at the courts of other Scandinavian rulers. The most magical of the skalds was Egil Skallagrímsson, a warrior and poet who is immortalized in *Egil's Saga*. A fierce, grim, and self-assertive warrior, he was also deeply versed in magical lore and produced touching poetry. It is possible that Egil composed and/or collected the poems that formed the Elder *Edda*.

THE RUNE POEMS

The rune poems are a later survival of runes as they appeared in medieval manuscripts, but they hold many keys to the runic tradition. There are at least three main rune poems—the Old English, Old Icelandic, and Norwegian rune poems. In each of these poems, there is a poetic stanza for every rune. The stanzas are quite mysterious and are useful for pondering on in meditations. The text of the poems is given in full in Chapter Seven, though verses are reproduced in relation to specific runes in Chapter Four.

CHANGES TO THE RUNE SYSTEM

The Viking age began in 793 C.E. with the raid on Lindisfarne in Northumbria. Then a period of raids and settlements followed, lasting until 1100 C.E. The changes that were occurring in pagan Scandinavian society at the time also brought changes to the runic system. The previously isolated nations came under economic, social, and religious pressure from the Christian south, as well as increasing their mobility with daring raids.

These changes had the effect of reducing the number of runes, yet much of the lore of the Elder Futhark was still preserved. Most of the famous rune inscriptions on stones in Norway, Sweden, and Denmark are in the new system that evolved, called the **Younger Futhark**. In recent times, the Younger Futhark runes have often been explored by modern groups inspired by or working in Scandinavia, such as the *Stav* martial art movement. Many of these inscriptions show evidence of magical practices and pagan religious practices.

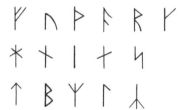

The Younger Futhark, above, and the Anglo-Saxon/Frisian Runes, right. In the contemporary runic revival, many people use these runes.

RUNES AND THE POPULAR IMAGINATION

The use of runes never really died—it just slumbered. Runes continued to be written in Iceland for many years, and the runic tradition survived in isolated rural folk settings and in the sophisticated magical and academic circles in Sweden, Norway, and Iceland.

In the 1870s, Richard Wagner presented the first performances of an epic fifteen-hour, four-opera production called *Der Ring des Nibelungen* (The Ring of the Nibelungs). Based on the German *Nibelungenlied*, a tragic poem, as well as on the *Eddas*, Wagner's piece was his own creation. He invented many of his myths, but from his work, the images of Odin, **Valkyries**, and **Loki** (see Chapter Three) reentered mainstream popular imagination.

The Hobbit by J. R. R. Tolkien was published in 1937 and introduced its many readers to the world of the runes. Tolkien fictionalized the Northern myths and added his own unique creations. The book featured runes on its cover and had a map mysteriously marked with runic script, as well as an introduction explaining the runes. With *The Hobbit* and later *The Lord of the Rings*, which features runes in its appendix, modern fantasy literature was brought into the mainstream. Tolkien's work inspired many to develop an interest in the runes.

Since the 1960s, esoteric themes have pervaded modern music, and there is virtually an entire subgenre of music inspired by Northern mythology, called "neo-folk," exemplified by UK band *Fire + Ice*. In the pop realm, waifish Icelander Björk is connected with the rune realms. Some of her lyrics have resonances of the pagan poetry of the North, and she sports a tattoo of a Helm of Awe (see Chapter Six), of the type called *Vegvisir* (Signpost). This sign is reputed to ensure that the wearer will never lose his or her way, even in storms or bad weather.

The current rune revival is into its second generation. Thousands of 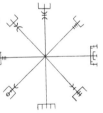 students of the runes have taken up the Elder Futhark and there are many reliable studies on the Elder tradition. Make use of this work and study. The modern runic revival (from the 1970s to date) is based on primary and secondary runic source material such as the archaeological, literary, and folkloric sources rather than on scriptures or imported belief systems.

Björk's *Vegvisir*

WORKBOOK EXERCISES

Visit your local library or bookstore and do some rune research. Use the books listed in Further Reading as a starting point. Record points of personal interest in your runic journal.

CHAPTER TWO

STARTING THE RUNIC QUEST

How to prepare for your work with the runes.

The previous chapter introduced you to the theory and history of the runes. In this chapter we will begin putting your study of the runic tradition into practice. Working with the runes requires time, effort, and concentration, but this will be rewarded. When you spend some time working with them, their presence will be made known in a myriad of ways—meaningful coincidences, greater inspirations, and a deeper understanding of your own life. The runes exist in all of our worlds. They symbolize archetypal, ancestral, and magical powers—and they are those powers themselves. The mysterious aspects of the runes exist in realms beyond our senses, but by working with them you can begin to understand these mysteries.

A NOTE ON INTERPRETING THE RUNES

Not all ways of looking at the runes will bring useful understanding. It is best to use the context of the old Northern tradition as your guide to understanding. Add to this your own persistent efforts, an approach that is open and receptive, and the practice of following both your reason and your intuition. As you learn, remember that the runes have individual personal meanings, so you cannot assume that your interpretation is valid for others and applies universally. Take your inspiration from the traditional way of seeing the runes. Learn the traditional meanings of the runes first, and later you will be able to reach a better personal understanding of the symbolism and power of each rune.

ENTERING THE RUNE WORLD

It takes work to become a rune worker, just as it takes work to become skilled in a trade, profession, or art. Practice is essential—and so is learning from our mistakes.

Learning the runes could be seen as a type of initiatory journey. On this journey the individual will be inducted into the lore of the runes and attain a new state of being. This is a journey in three stages:

1. *It takes the rune worker away from the everyday world.* When the rune worker begins to take up the study of the runes, separation occurs from the former, uninitiated self, and from family, friends, and others who are not seeking the runes.

2. *It allows the rune worker to focus on the runes and take them up,* absorbing them into his or her life. Taking up the runes will transform the seeker. The runes will increase self-awareness and promote the self-development of the individual.

3. *It returns the rune worker to the world enhanced by the runes,* which have now become part of his or her life. The initiated rune worker will have a more aware, dynamic, and integrated state of being and will be more knowledgeable about rune lore.

separation   reinclusion

transformation

Initiation

In the Northern tradition, various groups have their own rites for initiation. The process will differ, though some organizations standardize the initiation process for their members. Whatever path you choose, when you work with the runes in a serious way, you are taking them into your being—as Odin did.

CREATING A WORKING SPACE

Most religious and magical traditions set aside special places to perform their rituals. In the Elder runic tradition, a *Vé*—a holy place where religious and magical rites were enacted—was used. Many of these places were permanent sites or structures, and today many people are creating permanent rune-working sites once again.

However, a permanent structure is not necessary for those starting out in rune work. In this chapter you will learn how to prepare a working space using the Hammer Working practice inspired by the god **Thor** and how to hallow—make sacred—your working area.

THE HAMMER WORKING

The Hammer Working is designed to hallow your working space and all that is in it. It also is protective in that it protects rune workers from forces that seek to work against the runic mysteries. These forces are symbolized by the giants in Northern mythology, the **Etins**. Etins are not truly evil, but their single-minded pursuit of trying to disrupt the gifts and the worlds of the gods makes for eternal vigilance on the part of the mighty god of the hammer, Thor. In the Northern tradition, it is the god Thor who hallows important magical events and sacred rites with his magical hammer, Mjöllnir, which was created by the dwarves. It is beneficial to do something similar for your personal work. When you study the runes, not only are you making the myths come to life, you are also bringing the holy forms to work for you.

Thor is the most well-known god of the Northern world and is much loved. This is because as the defender of the gods and men, he tirelessly stands up for what is true. No longer seen as a god of human combat, he is viewed today as more of a patron of the people and, as such, is seen as unleashing his rage at those who would seek to put up barriers unjustly. As the "giant killer," he is useful to call upon if you are unfairly imposed upon by bureaucracies or other institutions.

Once you have worked through this chapter, perform a Hammer Working (page 30) to hallow your rune-working space.

Thor's hammer was the sign of those who were true to the Elder gods in the chaotic period leading up to the conversion of Scandinavia to Christianity. Many small Thor's hammer pendants have been found in the lands where people were true to the old ways. In the past century, the hammer has again become a popular symbol for those who embrace the old ways.

LEARNING AND DOING

To learn the wisdom of the runes and make this wisdom part of your own life, you will need to learn them through practice, experience, and time. As we all learn differently, there is no one set method for learning the symbolic meanings of the runes. Think about the learning methods you prefer as you begin your experience as a rune worker. Do you learn from reading and summarizing out of books? Do you prefer to have concepts demonstrated to you by way of pictures and diagrams? Do you learn best when listening?

Whichever is the best way for you to learn, you should be able to adapt learning the runes to your preferred method. Remember that people first learned the runes through the oral tradition. To learn in the same way today, look for books and music on the runes, and you may wish to join a rune-working group. See Resources, pages 184–185.

If you don't feel ready to interact with a group, you can still take advantage of learning by listening—you could record yourself reading the rune poems, inscriptions, or sagas. Play them back to help you remember them by heart. You will also find rune poems and inscriptions and the proper pronunciations on tape; see your local esoteric store.

 ## WORKBOOK EXERCISES

1. In your runic journal, list ten worthwhile things you have learned in the last two years.
2. What methods did you use to learn each of these things?
3. How can you apply these methods to rune learning?

BREATHING AND CONCENTRATING

Breath control is used in many disciplines, such as yoga, the martial arts, and meditation practices. Interestingly, breathing is the only involuntary bodily process that we can consciously control.

We often breathe incorrectly—too shallowly and too quickly—to keep up the pace of our busy world. Deep breathing will relax the body, reduce stress, and calm the mind. It will also make you receptive to the new worlds you will enter with your rune work.

 ## BREATHING EXERCISE

1. Find a quiet place with no television set or telephone within earshot. Sit comfortably, either cross-legged (a meditation cushion may be useful here), in a yoga position, or on a comfortable chair with your back straight and feet flat on the floor.
2. Breathe deeply, holding for four seconds. Then exhale, holding for four seconds.
3. Close your eyes and continue breathing in this manner for five minutes.
4. Feel the tensions melting away. Your body will become more relaxed. With the increase of oxygen, you will become more calm and more receptive to runic ideas.
5. Do this exercise daily.
6. Record your impressions in your runic journal.

CONCENTRATION

Concentration means focusing your thoughts and efforts fully upon some task. In the case of the runes, practicing your concentration will help you in many areas, from formulating questions to divination, practicing meditation on each of the runes, and general focus. Our world offers many distractions. Working with the runes can help to counter this approach and enable you to appreciate the wisdom of spending time on worthwhile goals.

EXERCISE TO INCREASE CONCENTRATION

1. First, do the breathing exercise described.
2. Then, using the Runic Table on page 47, copy the first rune, Fehu, into your runic journal or onto a piece of cardboard. Place it where you can see it from your meditation position.
3. Gaze at it intently, without straining your eyes, for two to four minutes.
4. Try to rid yourself of other thoughts during this time. If they arise, cast them off. Try to imagine them being flattened by a giant hammer.
5. Continue this exercise daily. Each time, select a new rune.
6. Record your experiences in your runic journal.

BEGINNING MEDITATION AND VISUALIZATION

Historical sources on runes and the Germanic heathen tradition do not refer to any particular type of meditation or similar mind tools. Yet these are important skills, common to many cultures, and helpful to those who study the runes because of the focus that they require and the separation from the busy world that they promote.

In the early days, rune workers probably practiced many of these skills, as theirs was an oral tradition and the lore would have had to be learned by heart. Similarly, skills in concentration and visualization would have been picked up in tasks such as working on traditional natural lore, practicing crafts from cooking to blacksmithing, and finding one's way without maps. Sciences such as astronomy and navigation would have required considerable skills of mind and memory.

MEDITATION

There are many styles of meditation. At this stage in your rune work, the main goal of meditation is to separate from the everyday world to bring the self into a calm, balanced state open to holistic experience. You may find the following two techniques useful.

SILENT MEDITATION

Find somewhere that is truly, not just bearably, quiet. If your house is not quiet enough, find a place in a local park, forest, or natural setting where you will not be disturbed.

1. Sit comfortably. If you can, sit cross-legged on the ground or floor. A firm, flat cushion may be useful. It is important to be comfortable. Some people prefer to meditate lying flat, but often this will lead to drowsiness or sleep. In the initial stages, try to meditate sitting up.

2. Breathe deeply (use the Breathing Exercise on page 26).

3. Relax. Starting with your toes and moving upward through your body, flex and then hold each set of your muscles for a few seconds. Then exhale, releasing your muscles and feeling the tension flow off you.

4. Once you are relaxed, keep focused on your breathing. You have calmed your body and now it is time to calm your mind. Let all worries flow away from you as you breathe out. Keep your mind in a state of receptive awareness. If any distracting thoughts arise, let them pass. There will be plenty of time later to return to resolve any issues. Stop the meditation only if there is an emergency.

5. Continue meditating for five to ten minutes. Increase the duration each time you do this meditation exercise. You will find it beneficial in many areas of your life and a useful precursor to runic work.

6. Write the results of each meditation in your runic journal.

RUNIC VOWEL MEDITATION

This meditation has a similar aim to the silent meditation opposite, but does not depend as much on your finding a peaceful spot. However, at the beginning stages of your rune work, it is always best to practice alone so you will not have the distractions of noise or curious onlookers.

1. Sit comfortably. Maintain a good posture, whatever your position.
2. Breathe deeply (use the Breathing Exercise on page 26).
3. Relax. Flex and release your muscles as you breathe deeply.
4. Still your mind. Close your eyes if this helps. Let your worries flow away so that you are in a receptive state.
5. With a resonant voice and as loudly as you are able to without disturbing others, intone the vowels of the runic row—u, a, i, e, o:

   Uuuuuuuuuuuuuuuuuuu.

   Aaaaaaaaaaaaaaaaaaaaaa.

   Iiiiiiiiiiiiiiiiiiiiiiiiiiiiiiiiiii.

   Eeeeeeeeeeeeeeeeeeee.

   Oooooooooooooooooo.

6. Keep the sounds distinct. Do not blend the vowels into each other. Cycle through the vowels. If you find one of these sounds particularly relaxing or conducive to meditation, focus on it for a while, but ensure that you do vocalize all of the vowels during this meditation.
7. Continue for five to ten minutes. Increase the duration each time you do the meditation. This meditation is also a useful precursor to runic work.
8. Record the experience of your meditation in your runic journal.

You may have learned meditation from other sources, as many other traditions have meditation practices. If you find these practices useful, adapt them for your rune work.

VISUALIZATION

Visualization means using the faculty of imagination to help create change within yourself. This process works by the conscious mental formation of imagery or concepts not available to the senses. Using this exercise, develop the skill of visualization and use it for rune work to retain in your mind the image of the rune you are working with.

VISUALIZATION EXERCISE

1. Select three or four small, distinctive objects.
2. Use a meditation technique to relax and focus yourself.
3. Pick up one of the objects, feel it, and study it from different angles for a few minutes until you think you have a good mental picture of it.
4. Cover it with a cloth or close your eyes. Try to picture the object in your mind's eye. Hold the image in your head for a few minutes.
5. Uncover the object and see if your visualization matches the real object.
6. Try to increase the time you can hold the mental image, up to a maximum of five minutes. For further visualization techniques see Further Reading, page 185.

HAMMER WORKING

Use this to practice the meditation and visualization exercises above:
1. Prepare by using the Silent or Runic Vowel Meditation (see pages 28–29). Face north. Trace the hammer sign (⊥) in the air in front of you. In your mind's eye, visualize a Thor's hammer being formed in the air before you, perhaps charged with glowing red. As you trace the sign, intone: "Hammer in the north, hold and hallow this stead."
2. Repeat for east, south, west, above, and below you. When you have done this, you will be warded by six mighty hammer signs—and will have created a protected environment ideal for your work. This will lessen any disturbances and encourage positive influences from the runes and the sacred beings of the runic worlds.

READING AND WRITING THE RUNES

Learning to read the runes is important. In *Egil's Saga*, Egil Skallagrímsson cautioned that "a man should not carve runes unless he knows well how to read." For Egil, this was illustrated by his encounter with the sick daughter of a farmer. A would-be rune worker had placed a rune stave that was wrongly composed in her bed, making her sicker. Egil destroyed the muddled runes and carved the correct runes, and then the girl felt well again.

This caution aside, do not hesitate to begin practicing writing the runes. However, if you do create any runic inscriptions anywhere other than in your runic journal, it may be a good idea to recycle them by letting them be subsumed by the elements (buried, burned, or immersed in water).

 WORKBOOK EXERCISES

1. Practice writing the Elder Futhark runes in your journal (see page 192). See the Runic Table on page 47. Keep them angular—there should not be any curves. After copying the runes one by one from the table, try copying them together, in order. Next, write your name and the names of your family members in runes.

   For example: ᛗᚷᛁᛚ ᛋᚲᚨᛚᚨᚷᚱᛁᛗᛗᛋᛟᚾ

2. Now try writing the names of the Northern gods and objects associated with them, such as Odin, Freyja, *Tyr*, mimung (sword), alu (ale, magical draught), and harrow (altar). For letters that do not exist in the runic system, substitute those with similar sounds, such as K for C.

   Try to write some runes daily. When you are able to read them as effortlessly as you can read English, you will know that their roots have been planted within you.

3. Update your runic journal (see page 12).

CHAPTER THREE

YGGDRASILL—THE RUNE WORLDS

Discover the mythological world of the runes and the powerful beings and lore associated with them.

THE INNER RUNE WORLD

Through your work in the early part of this book, you have begun to understand the external forms of the runes and have learned of their origins. You have been encouraged to create your own working space while you learn the runes. You have also learned, through meditation and other exercises, how to prepare your consciousness for a deeper understanding. It is the aim of this chapter to allow you to move into the inner realm of the runes—the mythic origins of the rune world and the powerful connections of the runes with the psychology of the human being.

We begin with a brief study of Northern mythology. Mythology works on many levels and particularly so in the rune world. The myths teach us the wisdom of our ancestors and give us heroic role models to aspire to, as well as inviting us to learn the lore of the heroes. We learn of figures such as Sigurd the dragon slayer, Egil the rune magician/poet, and Wayland the smith. Explore the mythic landscape of the rune worlds on as many levels as you can. See Further Reading on page 185 for recommended collections of the Northern myths.

MYTHIC BEINGS IN THE NORTHERN TRADITION

There are many beings in the Elder lore. These are some of the various types you will come across in your study of Northern mythology. The list includes the two families of the gods who were engaged in warfare in the early mythology. For an explanation of the mythical places named in this list, see the World Tree, pages 38–39.

FAMILIES OF THE GODS

The *Æsir* family contains mainly gods of consciousness, war, and government, the Highest and Holy Gods of Consciousness, of shaping the universe, and of ultimate potential. The ruling god of the Northern tradition is Odin.

The *Vanir* are mainly concerned with fertility and natural, worldly processes and cycles. The Rulers of the Vanir are Freyja and Freyr (the lady and the lord).

THE ÆSIR GODS

Odin (Odhinn, Woden, Wodan, Wuotan): Lord of runes, poetry, war, magic, ecstasy, awareness, the mind, the heroic dead. The All-Father. Sovereign god of the North. The most mysterious and changeable of the gods. He has one eye, as the other was sacrificed for Wisdom in Mimir's well. The day Wednesday is named after him, from "Wodens-day." See pages 36–37 for more about Odin.

Tyr (Tiwaz, Ziu): God of the sky, war, council, justice, and self-sacrifice. He sacrificed his hand in the binding of the *Fenris Wolf* so that the cosmic order could be protected. Tuesday is named after him.

Thor (Thórr, Donar): God of thunder, strength, and giant slaying. The most popular of the gods, Thor is the protector of the worlds of Northern mythology. His most recognizable attribute is the hammer Mjöllnir, which always returns after he has thrown it to devastating effect. While Odin is the god of rulers and magicians, Thor is the god who most of the Germanic farmer/warriors of the early days honored. Thursday is named after him.

Loki The trickster god. Loki is sly and deceitful and brings about necessary destruction so that rebirth can take place. Loki could be considered the "shadow side" of Odin.

THE VANIR GODS

Freyja The most important goddess of the Germanic myths. She is the beautiful god of love, fertility, eroticism, and the type of magic called *Seidhr* (see Chapter Six). The magical artifact associated with her is the Brisingamen necklace, which symbolizes her power over nature and cycles of all kinds. Friday is named after Freyja.

Freyr The most important Vanic god, a figure of Frith (peace), prosperity, and pleasure. Freyr is the fertility god and lord of harvests and worldliness, identified with the boar and hart. His weapon is a hart's horn.

OTHER BEINGS

Humans Recipients of the Gift of Consciousness. They inhabit the realm Midgard, where most meaningful action is manifested, and may also interact with the gods.

Valkyries "Choosers of the Slain"—heroic female warrior beings who live in *Asgard*. They may aid the chosen warrior or else escort him to *Valhalla* (a form of paradise).

Elves Bright, beautiful creatures that inhabit Ljossalfheim (Light-Elf World). Interactions with them are usually fortuitous and positive, although Anglo-Saxon tales do refer to them as sometimes causing illness to the unprepared.

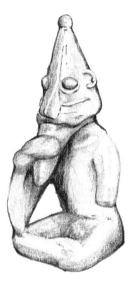

Freyr

Dwarves These are the "dark elves." Skillful and crafty, they create the magical weapons and objects of the Northern mythos.

Giants Often very ancient, unevolved forces. Sometimes (especially the Etin tribes) they act in opposition to the Gods of Consciousness.

Land-wights "Spirits of the place" who have a vested interest in particular locales. Can be beneficent or (rarely) malevolent.

Disir Protective matrons who aid in all aspects of childbirth and are possibly connected with the Valkyries.

Spawn of Loki The Æsir god Loki gave birth to many of the unique "monsters" of the North. These include the Fenris Wolf, Midgard Serpent, and even the helpful "best horse" *Sleipnir*, Odin's stead.

Norns The women of fate, the "weavers of destiny." (See Chapter Five for a description of the Greater Norns.)

ODIN, LORD OF THE RUNES

Odin is a mysterious god, wrapped in his great blue-black cloak, with his wide-brimmed hat and one eye burning fiercely, the other lost. He wields the spear Gungnir, which strikes as lightning. He is often mounted on his eight-legged horse, Sleipnir. About him fly his two ravens, Huginn (Mind) and Muninn (Memory). Odin seeks knowledge through all the realms. While he is extremely well traveled, he also sends forth his two ravens to collect information. Knowledge is sought where it can be found—Odin symbolizes the need to travel to new places and expand horizons. He also gazes upon the world from his vantage point on the high seat Hlidskjalf.

The most powerful god, Odin is not always the most popular. He is the god of mysterious areas with which many are uncomfortable, especially war, death, consciousness, wisdom, and magic.

Odin is the great god of the Teutonic worlds, known as All-Father. He has well over 170 names for his different aspects. These range from Grimnir (the Masked One) to Allfodhr (All-Father), or Bolverkr (Worker of Evil). Truly he is a god with many masks and facets. These names not only illuminate aspects of Odin, but also give hints about the religious and magical practices of his followers.

SYMBOLS OF ODIN'S WISDOM

Odin's wisdom comes from three major sources:

1. The rune initiation, where Odin sacrifices himself in order to win the secrets of the runes (see page 37).
2. The winning of the Poetic Mead. A giant had taken the magical mead made by dwarves from honey and the blood of Kvasir—a god who was created by the union of the Æsir and Vanir gods. Kvasir was exceedingly wise. Whoever drank the mead would be made a poet (the highest of the heathen arts). Odin restored the mead through a complex series of transformations and an exciting chase back to Asgard. On the way, he spilled a little mead and this is known as the share of which all poets partake.

3. Mimir's Well. Odin has mysterious connections with Mimir, an exceedingly wise, divine being. Mimir was killed in the dispute between the clans of the gods and Odin managed to preserve his head so that he could continue to ask Mimir's advice. Mimir also owned a well, which was the spring of Wisdom. Odin drank deeply from the well, but had to sacrifice his eye in order to do so.

TAKING UP THE RUNES

Odin wins the wisdom of the runes in his initiatory act of self-sacrifice on the World Tree.

> *I know that I hung*   *on a windy tree,*
>   *nights all nine,*
> *wounded by the spear*   *given to Odin,*
>   *myself to myself,*
> *on that tree*   *of which no man knoweth,*
>   *from whence its roots rises.*
> *They dealt me no bread*   *nor drinking horn,*
>   *I gazed down,*
> *I took up the runes*   *roaring I took them,*
>   *and fell back again.*

From "RÚNATALS" IN THE HÁVAMÁL, translation by Edred Thorsson

When we take up the runes in our own runic initiation, we are emulating Odin's act of taking up the runes.

YGGDRASILL, THE WORLD TREE

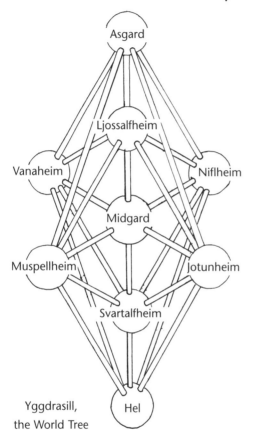

Yggdrasill,
the World Tree

There are Nine Worlds in the runic tradition:

- **Midgard**
- **Ljossalfheim**
- **Svartalfheim**
- **Vanaheim**
- **Jotunheim**
- **Muspellheim**
- **Niflheim**
- **Hel**
- **Asgard**

All of these worlds exist simultaneously and are connected by the World Tree, Yggdrasill. Yggdrasill means "Ygg's (Odin's) Horse," and is the basis of the Nine Worlds cosmology. Yggdrasill is the middle point of the worlds and a way of communication and travel between them. These worlds exist in an extradimensional sense, and models using our three dimensions can only roughly approximate. However, the image of the tree is useful for enabling us to understand these worlds.

Below is Hel, the realm of the dead. The crown of the tree is Asgard, the land of the gods. The trunk contains the most important world for us, Midgard, or Middle Earth. Just above Midgard is the realm of the elves, Ljossalfheim. And just beneath Midgard is Svartalfheim, the home of the dark elves, or dwarves. Arranged around the trunk are the worlds of Vanaheim (the home of the Vanir, gods of the natural world and fertility), and Jotunheim, the world of the giants. Muspellheim is the place of Cosmic Fire, and Niflheim the place of Cosmic Ice and Fog.

The most important of the runic worlds for the beginner rune worker to explore is Midgard—the world humans inhabit. This is the world of our families and friends, as well as our responsibilities, careers, and struggles. By trying to balance these appropriately, we will come to know the mysteries of Midgard. Runes will help to develop this balance.

BIRTH OF THE NINE WORLDS

Here is a brief overview of the mythic shaping of the Nine Worlds:

The universe was a holy and charged space called *Ginnungagap*—a potential waiting for energy. From Niflheim a stream of Cosmic Ice met its opposite in a stream of Cosmic Fire from Muspellheim. This collision caused an outpouring of energy, which crystallized into the great giant Ymir and its opposite, the great cow Audhumbla. The gods Odin, Vili, and Ve (Gods of Consciousness) were descended from the offspring of these two primal entities. The first conscious act these gods enacted was the shaping of the universe out of the body of Ymir, who was sacrificed to shape the universe into a more ordered state. The gods then created the Nine Worlds and humanity. It is interesting that in the myths, the gods created humans out of trees—the first male from an ash and the first female from an elm. They then gave them the Gift of Consciousness. Because of this, humans have a responsibility for their part in shaping the world, which is dynamic, ever in a state of being formed. Like the gods, we are responsible for our own actions. We can try to expand the forces of consciousness and safeguard our future or else get mired down in unproductive cycles and lose our way.

> *The Ash is the greatest and best of all trees. Its limbs stretch over the entire world and rise above heaven. Three roots of the tree hold it up and stretch out widely. One is among the Æsir, where Ginnungagap used to be, and the third in Niflheim.*
> GYLFAGINNUNG

BEINGS IN THE NINE WORLDS

Each of the worlds is populated by its own entities and beings. Some even live on the fringes of the inhospitable worlds of Cosmic Fire and Ice. These entities are sometimes referred to in mythological, runic, or religious contexts. The World Tree itself contains a number of entities, such as the eagle in the topmost branches, serpents in its roots, elks that live on the boughs, and a squirrel that stirs up trouble by passing insults from the serpents to the eagle.

RUNIC PSYCHOLOGY

Runes not only illuminate matters of cultural, theological, and magical importance, they are also well suited to exploring the inner mysteries of each of us—our selves. Self-exploration is of prime importance to rune workers, as self-knowledge is the starting point of true wisdom.

The runic universe is structured around the cosmic tree at the center of the worlds and the self is also connected to a tree. The first male and female were shaped from trees—the male from an ash, the female from an elm. In addition to giving them their natural, organic bodies, the gods gave them the Gift of Consciousness. In the *Edda* myth of *Voluspá* 17–18, Odin and his hypostases (aspects) are described as the shapers of the self complex:

> *Óthin gave Önd (vital breath)*
> *Hœnir gave mind,*
> *Löthur gave art*
> *and good complexion.*
> VOLUSPÁ 17–18

The Northern vision of the self was of a multifaceted entity. It was a holistic view. The various parts of the self were carefully categorized. The body—the physical aspect—was considered as important a part of the individual as the metaphysical aspects such as inspiration. Becoming a more integrated person and more aware of who we are and of all of our faculties and potentials is a sacred task of the rune worker.

RUNIC SOUL LORE

As you look at the runes in the next chapter, you will learn about different aspects of the self in the runic worldview. It is useful to begin this study by examining the Rune Gild's approach to the self. The Gild sees the self as a ninefold model, with all nine aspects based on traditional descriptions. The interaction of these nine parts make up the self:

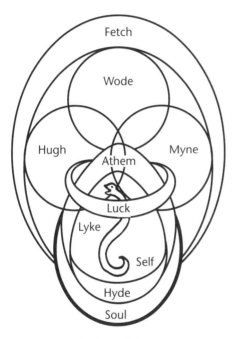

Runic soul lore

1. *Shade*—soul
2. *Lyke/Lich*—body
3. *Hyde*—shape of body
4. *Hugh*—intellectual/analytical aspects
5. *Myne*—reflective, memories, ancestral aspects
6. *Athem*—breath of life
7. *Wode*—inspiration
8. *Fetch*—storehouse of images, warden
9. *Hamingja*—personal power, luck, guardian spirit

The rebirth of runic soul lore has been quickened by the work of holistic psychologists such as Carl Jung. Once you have completed your initial studies, you will find much of interest in Jung's works to intensify your knowledge of the runes.

The ninefold structure of the runic soul lore is symbolized by the symbol of the Valknut, which is associated with Odin and is also a sign of the modern Gild.

THE RUNIC SOUL LORE IN YOUR LIFE

You can apply the runic soul lore to your life in the following ways. You can:

1. Integrate becoming physically healthy or maintaining your health with rune work. (Using the Lyke.) Some of the activities in this book have been set specifically to promote your physical health.
2. Trace your ancestors and relate them to yourself (Myne).
3. Learn to balance logical and creative skills (Hugh and Myne).
4. Increase and focus your inspiration (Wode).
5. Change your perceptions of your body (Hyde).
6. Think about what happens after death (Shade, Fetch, Self).
7. Investigate Jungian archetypes (Myne and all).
8. Focus your will (Self, Hugh, and Myne).
9. Know yourself and become who you are meant to be (all).

 WORKBOOK EXERCISE

1. Write in your runic journal your thoughts about:
   - each of the Nine Worlds,
   - Midgard, the most important world for humanity, and
   - how humans should treat the world they live in—Midgard—knowing that it is a sacred place.
2. Visit a local forest, garden, or park.
   - Reflect on the Nine Worlds and the World Tree that connects them.
   - What type of trees are you drawn to? Find out their names.
   - Later, find a seed or sapling of that type of tree and plant it on a special occasion.
3. Practice the Meditation on the World Tree (see page 43).
4. Update your runic journal (see page 12).

MEDITATION ON THE WORLD TREE

This meditation makes use of the work you have done in earlier chapters, using both the Runic Vowel Meditation (page 29) and the Hammer Working (page 30):

1. Begin with the Hammer Working.
2. Next, visualize a great ash or evergreen tree. Using the diagram on page 38 as a guide, visualize Asgard at the top of the tree. Using your skills learned in Rune Vowel Meditation, intone **Aaaaaaaaa** three or nine times while you are visualizing Asgard. Try to keep an impression of Asgard (and the other worlds) in your memory for writing in your runic journal.
3. At the bottom of the tree, at the lowest roots, visualize Hel. Intone **Uuuuuuuuu** three or nine times.
4. One-fifth of the way down the tree from Asgard, visualize Ljossalfheim. Intone **Eeeeeeeee** three or nine times.
5. One-fifth of the way up the tree from Hel, and below the surface of the ground, visualize Svartalfheim. Intone **Iiiiiiiii** three or nine times.
6. At the center of the tree, visualize Midgard. Intone **Ooooooooo** three or nine times.
7. Orbiting around Midgard on a horizontal plane, visualize the four worlds in order—Vanaheim, Jotunheim, Muspellheim, and Niflheim. Intone their names three times each.
8. Return your visualization to Midgard and intone **Ooooooooo** three to nine times. While in Midgard, take particular note of the way the roots of the World Tree are woven subtly into the fabric of the world. Midgard is our dwelling place, the real world, and it is the land where our ideals have to be enacted with objective action.

Practice this meditation daily until you no longer need to refer to your notes of the World Tree diagram. Then use it whenever you would like to think about the cosmology of the World Tree. As you become more proficient with runes, revisit this exercise and explore the other worlds with your questions and insight.

CHAPTER FOUR

THE FUTHARK—THE RUNIC SYSTEM

Learn about each rune and its essential meaning.

ABOUT THE ELDER FUTHARK RUNES

This book focuses on the earliest of the rune scripts, known as the Elder Futhark. This is a useful knowledge base for the later rune rows that developed from the Elder Futhark (see the Younger Futhark and the ***Anglo-Saxon/Frisian Runes***, page 20). The rune names were not recorded in manuscripts until comparatively late—between the ninth and the fourteenth centuries. However, the rune names of the Elder Futhark have also been reconstructed and we will learn of them here as they help us to understand what the runes mean.

The runes are more than just a curious angular script. Each rune has a distinctive name that symbolizes the mysteries and secrets contained within it. For example, the "F" rune has the name "Fehu," which means "cattle" or "mobile property," and the rune points to the importance of the wealth symbolized by these things when setting out on a quest or getting ready for action. See page 47 for a list of the rune names and their meanings.

You have already been practicing writing the runes. This chapter is designed for you to gain a deeper grasp of the runes, as well as providing some ways you can broaden your horizons as you uncover each rune mystery. Practical exercises will help you to make the runes a part of your life.

APPROACHING THE RUNES

Although our knowledge base of the Elder workings of the runic system is incomplete, the primary sources for the tradition include:

• the twenty-four runes,

• rune inscriptions,

• the rune poems, and

• the *Eddas*.

These primary sources form the basis of the tradition. When investigating this tradition and putting it to use, you will need to combine a rational approach, based on these sources, with intuition and with your subjective sense of beauty, magic, and pragmatism. The objective sources are very important, especially when we begin studying the runes. When the Elder tradition is known and worked with, the hidden doors to the inner mysteries of the runes will be easier to open.

As with the old Germanic art forms, the runes are interwoven with beings, gods and men, fantastic animals, dragons, and other elements of the mythological world. Refer to Chapter Three for details about these elements. The runes are also linked with one another—in many cases the knowledge of one rune will help us to understand another. The runes lead one on an inner journey, and one rune leads to another. There is a spiritual journey as we move from one rune to the next.

The important thing to remember is that the knowledge of the runes cannot be instilled from outside—it must be won anew by each rune initiate. This can be daunting to the rune learner, but because each rune, each myth, and each element of the system is connected in some way, just by starting to learn the runes and actively putting them to work will lead you from one rune to the next.

CHARACTERISTICS OF THE RUNES

Each rune has four important characteristics:

1. Physical shape
2. Number
3. Name
4. Sound

These characteristics are interlinked. They combine to give the runes their complex symbolic meaning.

Bind runes are runes that are joined together or overlap in some way for apparently magical reasons—thus linked they act as a powerful combination of their individual forces.

RUNE NAMES

The rune names are significant. In English, the letters have no names, only a phonetic sound—"ay, bee, see," and so on. The only alphabets to have meaningful names for their letters are the runes, Hebrew, and the Celtic Ogham script. The rune names contain the sound of the rune, as well as the idea. The name in most cases starts with the rune sound, as in **A**-nsuz and **T**-iwaz, for example, but in the case of the Z rune, it is at the end: Elha-**Z** (see pages 110–113).

The names are an important aspect of the esoteric lore of the runes. They name the central symbol of each rune. For example, "Fehu" means "cattle." This can indicate actual cattle (very important for an agriculture-based people) or a symbol of "mobile wealth"— gold, fine arts and crafts, or similar objects. The complete list of Futhark rune names, along with their meanings, is given in the table on page 47. In the detailed explanations of the runes from pages 54 to 149, the symbolic meanings of the names are explored in some depth.

WORKBOOK EXERCISE

Speak aloud each rune in sequence, until you are comfortable with each sound.

RUNE NAMES AND PRONUNCIATION

RUNE	NAME	ENGLISH LETTER	ENGLISH PRONUNCIATION	TRANSLATION OF NAME
ᚠ	Fehu	F	feh-who	Cattle
ᚢ	Uruz	U	oor-ooze	Aurochs
ᚦ	Thurisaz	TH	thoor-isaz	Thurs (giant)
ᚨ	Ansuz	A	awn-sooz	Ancestral God
ᚱ	Raidho	R	rye-though	Ride
ᚲ	Kenaz	K	kain-az	Torch
ᚷ	Gebo	G	geh-bo	Gift
ᚹ	Wunjo	W	wuhn-yo	Joy
ᚺ	Hagalaz	H	hagh-alaz	Hail
ᚾ	Nauthiz	N	nowth-is	Need
ᛁ	Isa	I	ee-sa	Ice
ᛃ	Jera	J	yair-a	Year
ᛇ	Ihwaz	EI	ayhh-waz	Yew
ᛈ	Perthro	P	pairth-row	Lot Box
ᛉ	Elhaz	Z	el-haz	Elk
ᛋ	Sowlio	S	so-willow	Sun
ᛏ	Tiwaz	T	tee-waz	Tyr (a god)
ᛒ	Berkano	B	bear-kano	Birch
ᛖ	Ehwaz	E	ehh-waz	Horse
ᛗ	Mannaz	M	man-naz	Man
ᛚ	Laguz	L	lagh-ooze	Lake
ᛜ	Ingwaz	NG	ing-waz	Ing (a god)
ᛞ	Dagaz	D	dagh-az	Day
ᛟ	Othala	O	owe-thala	Ancestral Property

RUNE NUMBERS

Begin by learning the runes in order and learning their numbers, which run in sequence, at the same time. Learning the numbers is fairly straightforward—just follow the path of the runes from 1 to 24. The numerical order is further divided into three "families" of the runes, called the *Aettir*, or "eights." These three groups of eight runes are known as "Freyr's Eight," "Hagal's Eight," and "Tyr's Eight."

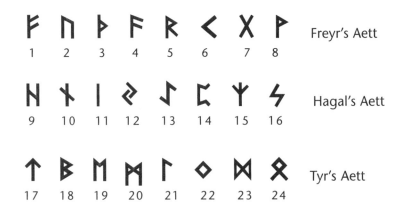

1	2	3	4	5	6	7	8	Freyr's Aett
9	10	11	12	13	14	15	16	Hagal's Aett
17	18	19	20	21	22	23	24	Tyr's Aett

THE THREE GROUPS

There is no apparent linguistic reason why the runes are arranged in three groups of eight. However, this proved extremely useful for the Elder rune masters, especially when they wanted to "hide" their inscriptions (make them more mysterious and therefore more runically charged). They could use the Aettir system as an extra level of numerical code. As an example, they could use other runes, marks, or codes to refer to "line 1, rune 2." This is what they did with the Körlin Rune Ring, which has the inscription **ALU**, and then a bind rune that is both A and L, but which through a code of "line 1, rune 2" signifies U.

The ALU
bind rune

The runes may have been broken into groups of three to reflect the traditional threefold structure of the rune gilds: learner, fellow, and master. With this structure, the path of the rune learner would be to travel from the first rune in the first row, Fehu, to the last, Wunjo—a path from "power" to "joy."

ALU MEDITATION

The bind rune ALU (ale), mentioned on page 48, means an inspired or ecstatic force. Mead and honey ales were considered potent drinks, and the process of brewing was thought to be a gift from above. The formula ALU is used to raise an inspired force and to use that force for protection or other purposes.

1. Focus yourself using the Silent Meditation on page 28.
2. Draw or carve the ALU bind rune (see Chapter Five for instructions on carving).
3. Visualize a stream of force empowering the carving or picture of the bind rune. While you do so, intone the following Galdra, or chant:

   Ansuz Laguz Uruz
   ALU ALU ALU (three times)
   AAALLLUUU (three times)
   ALU

4. Meditate on how you can use the inspiration you have raised—perhaps to ward your working space, finish a task that needs doing, or overcome personal fetters.
5. Write your impressions in your runic journal.

NUMBER LORE

The runic tradition has numerological aspects, though the rune number system differs in some ways from the more popular Western numerology. Systematic studies of the numerology of the runes have been few but thorough (see Further Reading, page 185). The number lore underpinning the runes adds an extra dimension to analyzing rune inscriptions, formulas, and spells. The table below presents a summary of the symbolic meanings of numbers in the rune system, along with an example of each.

You are most likely to find the applications of 3, 9, and 24 useful in the initial stages of your rune learning. You can also become sensitized to the use of numbers in rune work by recording in your runic journal any instance of a significant number you find while studying the runes. As your studies develop, so too will your understanding of the symbolic meanings of numbers in the runic system.

Number	Meaning	Example
1	Beginnings	The Giant Ymir
2	Cooperation	The two ravens of Odin—Huginn & Muninn
3	Holiness, process	The Three Norns—Urdhr, **Verdhandi**, Skuld
4	Solid mass, steady power	The four dwarves at the edges of the world
5	Order	The days of the week, named after the gods
6	Vibrant life	The hex signs
7	Death/otherworld	The complete week
8	Complete manifestation, symmetry	Waiting eight nights for betrothment
9	Transformation, most holy, cosmological significance	Odin's nine nights on the World Tree in the *Hávamál*
24	The complete Futhark. Mystery made manifest in the world	The twenty-four runes

RUNE SHAPES

The shapes of the runes—their visual aspect—form one of the keys to their secrets. Most people are struck by the stark angular shapes of the runes. There is a maxim among many rune workers: "If it looks like a rune, then it may have runic effects." This can apply to many forms of human-made or natural phenomena. Look for runic shapes in trees, architecture, art, design, and traditional folk items.

This book uses the standard shapes of the Elder Futhark, but there are variants for most of the runes. These variants may be important for particular inscriptions, in that they may focus the energy of the runes in a different manner. Runes with the most variants are Jera and Sowilo. You will see these on pages 99 and 115.

Individual rune carvers often had their own styles. This is especially apparent in the rune stones in Denmark and Sweden from the later Viking age. From the earliest stages the rune shapes were well defined and carving techniques highly skillful. As in most areas of life, however, some carvers were better at the task than others. Some created beautiful art, while others worked with a functional purpose. Both are valid approaches.

RUNE SOUNDS

While the shape and names of the runes are important aspects of their mysteries, the actual sounds of the runes are important too. When Odin took up the runes, he is said to have "taken them up screaming." This indicates that there is a sonic key to the runes.

In oral traditions, sound is extremely important. In today's world of text and disjointed electronic communication, speech, song, and chant are devalued. To understand the resonance of the runes beyond their mere textual values, we need to appreciate them as spoken, sung, and "roared." The sonic aspects of the runes are released through Galdra—this means "magic," especially that which is verbal or sound-based (see Chapter Six).

There are many events in our lives where words themselves, as well as acts, have a symbolic significance and in themselves constitute an action. For instance, we seal a marriage vow with a verbal agreement and we give binding verbal oaths in court.

The runes were spoken in all of the Germanic/Scandinavian languages. Many rune workers aspire to learn at least one of these older languages. This can be a long and hard task—although with tangible rewards. Speaking another language can help you to understand the context of the runes and may also help on many other levels—scientific research indicates that learning other languages can increase mental capacity.

A KEY TO THE RUNES

In the pages that follow, you can explore each rune in some depth. Here are some of the categories covered and an explanation of them.

Rune name The reconstructed name of the Elder Futhark rune.

Meaning The meaning of the name in English.

Shape The standard shape of the rune.

Alternative shape Less common, alternative shapes for the rune.

Keywords A summary of what the rune means on an esoteric level, helpful for divination.

Rune poem stanzas The relevant stanzas from the rune poems. See Chapter Seven for these poems in full. The poems are abbreviated as follows: **OERP** for the Old English Rune Poem; **ONRP** for the Old Norwegian Rune Poem; and **OIRP** for the Old Icelandic Rune Poem.

Meaning An in-depth account of the symbolic meaning of each rune. Use this for your own rune work and as a starting point for further research.

Galdra (chanting the rune for magical purposes). These Galdra have been prepared with the rune learner in mind. To intone them, find a level of utterance comfortable for your voice. Intone clearly. Keep each sound clear rather than blending the sounds. Experiment with quick and slow versions. Slow chanting will allow you to reflect on the sound and the rune.

Magical uses Modern uses for the runes in magical work (see Chapter Six).

Things to do Cultural activities you can use to experience the rune in your life.

WORKBOOK EXERCISES

1. Reflect on the shape of the runes. See the list on page 47. Which rune shape seems to speak to you? Meditate on this shape. Now read the explanation for that rune, writing down your responses to what you read in your runic journal. For example:
   - What resonance does this rune have in your life right now?
   - Did you expect to be drawn to this rune? Why or why not?
   - In what types of situations can you see yourself embracing the energies of this rune?

2. As you work through this chapter, ask the following five questions of each rune. Use a meditation or visualization exercise to help you. Record your experiences in your runic journal.
   - What does this rune mean to me?
   - How can it further my goals?
   - How can this rune show my blind spots?
   - What do I understand best about this rune?
   - What should I try to understand better about this rune?

3. For each rune, also ask the same questions about the rune poem extract (the rune poems are given in full in Chapter Seven):
   - What does this poem mean to me?
   - How can it further my goals?
   - How can this poem show my blind spots?
   - What do I understand best about this poem?
   - What should I try to understand better about this poem?

4. Update your runic journal (see page 12).

FEHU

Name Fehu—Wealth, cattle, gold

Alternative shape ⟨

Number 1

Keywords Rune of energy and wealth (gold). The rune of new journeys. Circulation of energy, wealth, and power.

Rune poem stanzas

(Wealth) is a comfort to   every man
although every man ought   to deal it out freely
if he wants, before the lord,   his lot of judgment
OERP

F (Gold) causes strife among kinsmen;
*   the wolf grows up in the woods.*
ONRP

F (Gold) is strife among kinsmen   and fire of the flood tide
*   and the path of the serpent.*
Gold.   *"Leader of the war-band"*
OIRP

MEANING

Fehu is the rune of energy and wealth. It enables you to begin new journeys. It is the first rune and is therefore useful for starting your quest to master the mysteries. In Fehu is found life, wealth, and luck. As the rune of the Cosmic Fire streaming toward the Cosmic Ice, Fehu can help set things in motion. Fehu is the ring of fire we must dare to pass through if we are really to seek the mysteries. All beginnings are exciting and sometimes seem dangerous.

The later rune poems show the connection of this rune with the mystery of wealth. But just using runes will not make us wealthy. The Fehu rune in the poems tells us that we have to "circulate" money and our skills—to "deal them out freely."

Getting your finances together is a good step to undertake while meditating on Fehu. As with all works of magic in the world, you need to work practically in the human world; you cannot expect heaps of gold to appear suddenly. You will need to work more on areas that already supply you with an income or even on a hobby that could become lucrative. Perhaps this rune could help you turn your weekend pastime into a viable business.

Fehu is about mobile wealth rather than property. Keep this rune in mind when you are thinking about shares, stocks, bonds, and other "mobile" investments. It also urges us to circulate our wealth in order to acquire an increase in power. We need to share knowledge and to network if we want to learn new skills and gain allies.

Too much of this rune can lead to burnout. It is a reminder that the rune worker can take on too much by becoming immersed in rune studies and that it is a good idea to take a break every so often.

To use the mysteries of Fehu, enact them in your everyday life. Create opportunities for yourself. Seek the mysteries and speak about what you find.

FEHU EXERCISES

Galdra
Fehu Fehu Fehu
Feeeeeeeee
Fe-Fe-Fe-Fe
Fu-Fu-Fu-Fu
Fehu Fehu Fehu

Magical uses
• Increase in wealth
• Increase in social standing

Things to do
1. Give gold jewelry to someone special.
2. Share what you know—a skill, a craft, a form of knowledge.

Thoughts to meditate upon
Use each of these questions as a focus for a meditation session. When the session is over, record in your runic journal the answers that emerged from the meditation.
1. How does wealth come my way?
2. How can I keep it circulating to me?
3. Why does "gold cause strife among kinsmen?"

Three ways to enact Fehu in your life
1. Sell something. Invest the money you make from this sale.
2. What do you enjoy doing? How can you maintain or increase your wealth by doing what you enjoy?
3. Listen to or attend a performance of Wagner's opera *Rheingold*.

URUZ

Name Uruz—Aurochs

Alternative shapes ⋀⋂⋒

Number 2

Keywords Rune of strength and vitality. Rune of organic transformation.

Rune poem stanzas

(Urus) is fearless   and greatly horned
a very fierce beast   it fights with its horns,
a famous roamer of the moor   it is a courageous animal.
OERP

U (Slag) is from bad iron;
*   oft runs the reindeer on the hard snow.*
ONRP

U (Drizzle) is the weeping of clouds and the lessener of the rim of ice
*   and the herdsman's hate.*
Shadow, or Shower.   "Leader"
OIRP

MEANING

Uruz is the rune of strength and vitality. It is also the rune of organic transformation, particularly the maintenance of good health. Health is maintained by exercise such as "roaming," or running, as in the rune poems, having a correct diet, and ensuring a safe environment. Uruz also promotes healing for those who have been ill and is good to call upon any time strength is required. Uruz is an ordering process. It symbolizes the meeting of Fire and Ice (see page 39), which gave great impetus to the mythic creation of the Nine Worlds.

The rune symbolizes the horns of the great (now extinct) aurochs, a type of European bison famed for its strength and might. The cow is considered holy in many traditions, as it gives sustenance, and also, in the Germanic myths, helped in the forming of the universe.

It is also the rune of defense through might and is a vital power, best explored and practiced in times of Frith (peace) so that it can be called upon quickly in times of dire need. Uruz is a rune of overwhelming power and dynamic action, especially action for the swift defense of all the worlds. It represents the physical and mighty acts that are necessary to prepare for and mete out defensive actions. Uruz combines well with other runes—for example, with Othala, when defense of the homeland is needed. The danger is that defensiveness, when either unwarranted or unchecked, or not used wisely, can lead to excessive vigilance, and the individual can be stressed either by an obsession with control or by becoming too defensive.

In the heathen "tool kit" the ox is associated with the drinking horn, an essential piece of equipment for those wanting to reconstruct the religion of their ancestors. At feasts, mead or ale would be ceremonially drunk—guests would either drink to each other's health with "wassail," or in the more ceremonial *sumble*, a sacred drinking ritual.

Uruz is extremely useful for investigating the paths and ways to which we are innately predisposed. Through fearless strength we can overcome many obstacles. Uruz is the force that turns walls on our paths into doors.

The horseshoe we sometimes place over our doors for good luck is shaped like this rune and has its symbolic power.

URUZ EXERCISES

Galdra
Uruz Uruz Uruz
UUUUUUUUU
UUUUUUUUU
Ur-Ur-Ur-Ur
Uruz Uruz Uruz

Magical uses
• Health maintenance and healing
• Attracting good fortune

Things to do
1. Make a drinking horn.
2. Participate in a friendly sport, one that tests strength, such as wrestling.
3. Create a home-brewed ale or mead to put in your drinking horn.

Thoughts to meditate upon
1. What is my best physical talent?
2. Can I increase my strength?
3. If I were fearless, what would I do differently?

Three ways to enact Uruz in your life
1. Exercise daily. Devise exercises that will strengthen you.
2. Evaluate your self-defense skills. If necessary, bring them up to the level you think necessary.
3. Place a horseshoe over a door in your home to encourage good luck to enter.

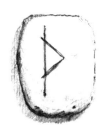

THURISAZ

Name Thurisaz—Thurs, Giant

Alternative shape ▷

Number 3

Keywords Rune of the will, resistance, and Thor. Rune of an opposing force.

Rune poem stanzas

> TH (Thorn) is very sharp;   for every thegn
> who grasps it, it is harmful   and exceedingly cruel
> to every man   who lies upon it.
> OERP

> TH (Thurs) causes the sickness of women;
>   few are cheerful from misfortune.
> ONRP

> TH (Thurs) is the torment of women   and the dweller in the rocks
>   and the husband of the Etin-wife Vardh-runa.
>   Saturn.   "Ruler of the Legal Assembly"
> OIRP

MEANING

Thurisaz is the rune of the will, the god Thor, and his hammer Mjöllnir. It is the rune of force and will. Thurisaz fights fire with fire. It is a reactive force. There is danger inherent in Thurisaz. It may indicate enemies acting against your purposes or a betrayal. Thurisaz may also signify bad relations with members of the opposite sex or unconscious compulsions that are hard to control.

In the Germanic tradition, the giants frequently sought to destroy the work of the gods. In return, Thor sought to smash giants with his hammer. He was the original "giant killer" and this was one of his favorite sports. Thor was not only the strongest of the gods, he was also the most popular. He was the exemplary god of the warrior/farmer, which was the occupation of most people in the European preindustrial era. Thor was always dependable, always predictable. Although not as clever as the other gods, he was the one to whom everyone could relate. Also, because he was in charge of thunder, Thor was in control of the weather and therefore important to farmers. Legends of Thor made popular entertainment, as he seemed always to get himself into tricky situations and have to complete near-impossible tasks. Among others, he had to fish for the World Serpent, wrestle Old Age, and dress up in a bridal outfit to try to get his hammer back from a thieving giant.

Thurisaz is the way of pure action—of will. This is not preplanned or conscious action, but the innate, unconscious forces or impulsiveness. This is characteristic of the giant's ways of thinking—giants were seen not as evil, but as destructive because they were so single-minded and so incapable of evolving their perspective. Thor reacts quite predictably to any sign of giants, brandishing his hammer and chasing them off. Thurisaz can be used to control unconscious forces by harnessing them against opposing forces. It breaks opposition and maintains order through active defense.

Thurisaz is also the sleep-thorn, in the form of a spindle, which put Sleeping Beauty into a state of slumber from which she could only be awakened by her prince. The thorn can also be used to awaken a person from slumber. In the heathen version of "Sleeping Beauty," "the Lay of Sigdrífa," the Valkyrie, after being awoken by Sigurd, tells that she was put to sleep by "sleep runes."

THURISAZ EXERCISES

Galdra
Thurisaz Thurisaz Thurisaz
Thur-Thur-Thur
Thi-Thi-Thi-Thi
Tha-Tha-Tha-Tha
Thurisaz Thurisaz Thurisaz

Magical uses
- Active defense: being prepared for trouble
- Destruction (neutralization) of enemies
- Awakening the will

Things to do
1. Make or purchase a Thor's hammer to wear. Hallow it with the Hammer Working on page 30.

Thoughts to meditate upon
1. What does Thor mean to me?
2. When is my will strongest?
3. What is my greatest misfortune and how do I live with it?

Three ways to enact Thurisaz in your life
1. Practice the Hammer Working on page 30.
2. Research Thor. Why was he so popular?
3. Do something active with a hammer. Build something.

ANSUZ

Name Ansuz—God, chieftain

Alternative shape ⌐

Number 4

Keywords Rune of the mind, self-consciousness, and rune work. The rune of the god Odin.

Rune poem stanzas

A (God) is the chieftain   of all speech,
 the mainstay of wisdom   and comfort to the wise,
 for every noble warrior   hope and happiness.
OERP

A (Estuary) is the way of most journeys;
    but the sheath is (that way) for swords.
ONRP

A (Ase) is the olden-father   and Asgards chieftain
         and the leader of Valhalla.
  Jupiter.   "Point-Leader"
OIRP

MEANING

Ansuz is the rune of the mind, self-consciousness, and rune work. Ansuz encourages you to wisely develop in all the realms of knowledge. It is also the rune of Odin, the great god of the North. It is the rune of awareness, inspiration, and communication. Ansuz contains and expresses the runic forces that are hallmarks of the myths of Odin.

Odin discovered and understood the runes through his self-sacrifice on the World Tree (see Chapter Three). This is reported in *Hávamál 138*:

Wounded by the spear, given to Odin,
 Myself to myself…
Then began I to grow and gain in insight,
 to wax also in wisdom:
one word led on to another word,
one work led on to another work.
HÁVAMÁL 138

In this moment of extreme consciousness (sacrificing himself to himself), Odin took up the runes, which had previously been hidden. It is this mythic event that has made it possible for us humans to seek and understand the runes. The runes are not static—they have a mission to lead us from one work to the next work—to grow in wisdom and self-integration.

The passing of this gift to humans along ancestral lines is detailed in the *Edda* poem *Lay of Hyndla*. This feature is also apparent in the indigenous Anglo-Saxon heathen version of Odin—Woden, whose name heads the genealogy lists of royalty well after conversion to Christianity. In this respect Ansuz is a rune to call on for all interested in family history.

As the rune of inspiration, Ansuz can be used to call upon for all matters concerning poetry, writing, and arts. Poetry was especially prized as an art form in the Germanic world. Skalds, or poets, were held in high repute and could even get themselves out of death sentences through the clever use of poetry to shift the rulers' attitudes (a famous example is Egil Skallagrímsson's "Head Ransom" poem).

ANSUZ EXERCISES

Galdra

Ansuz Ansuz Ansuz

AAAAAAAAA

An-An-An-An

Au-Au-Au-Au

Ansuz Ansuz Ansuz

Magical uses

- Increase of magical skills
- Communication skills
- Inspiration

Things to do

1. Learn a Northern language, such as Old English, German, Icelandic, or Old Norse.
2. Recite poetry.
3. Commit the rune poems to memory.

Thoughts to meditate upon

1. What makes me most inspired?
2. How do I communicate best? How can I improve?
3. What does "wisdom" mean to me?

Three ways to enact Ansuz in your life

1. Seriously follow an inspiration.
2. Read some runic or *Edda* poetry to your friends or family.
3. Learn better communication skills.

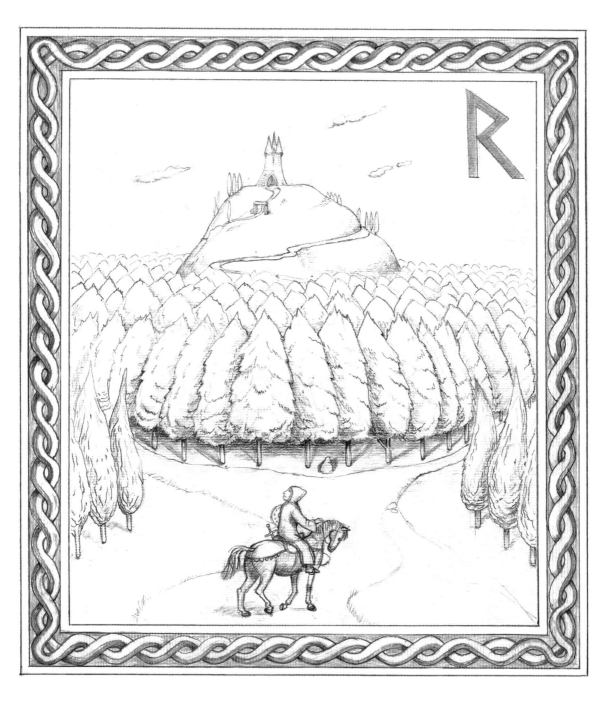

RAIDHO

Name Raidho—Riding

Alternative shapes ᚱ ᚱ

Number 5

Keywords Rune of right order. The right way to proceed. Rune of reason, rationality, and progress.

Rune poem stanzas

R (Riding) is in the hall,   to every warrior
easy, but very hard   for one who sits up
on a powerful horse   over the miles of road.
OERP

R (Riding), it is said, is the worst for horses;
    Reginn forged the best sword.
ONRP

R (Riding) is a blessed sitting   and a swift journey
         and the toil of the horse.
   Journey.   "Worthy-man"
OIRP

MEANING

Raidho is the rune of riding. Develop balance and be reasonable. Riding is an acquired skill. To be a good rider, you need to consider the horse (see Ehwaz, pages 126–129), your balance, the environment, and where you are going. Similarly, in using Raidho you need to be aware of your environment, both physical and emotional.

Raidho represents the goal of good counsel, of the right way. This way is found by rationally considering the situation and weighing up a course of action based on both reason and traditional ways. In the old Germanic world, deeds spoke louder than words and people were ultimately accountable for their deeds that affected others. If they broke the laws of the community, they were outlawed—that is, not under the protection of the law. Oaths were considered extremely binding. Oath breaking was a serious offense and an oath breaker was considered to have blighted his or her being.

Raidho is inextricably linked with ritual, especially in relation to the correct way to perform. While many of the magical aspects of the Northern ways were down to earth and probably only enacted when needed, the *things*, or legal assemblies, and seasonal religious ceremonies of the North were held at the proper times with great pride and dedication.

Religious ceremonies include those for particular gods or for Winter Nights, Yule, and Easter. In addition, marriages, funerals, and naming ceremonies were all religious events with their own special customs and expected performances. A priesthood existed, based in the more established temples in the Germanic world, to ensure the correct performance of these rites. In the temples, oath rings were kept and binding oaths were sworn on these. Breaking an oath was going against all that was right.

Raidho is the rune of regular rhythmic action, not just in religion but also in song, dance, music, poems, and performance. In the realm of wisdom it is the regular "taking stock" of oneself, when untrue ideas, attitudes, and notions are discarded.

RAIDHO EXERCISES

Galdra
Raidho Raidho Raidho/RRRRRRRRR/Ra-Ra-Ra-Ra/Ri-Ri-Ri-Ri/Ro-Ro-Ro-Ro/Raidho Raidho
  Raidho

Magical uses
• Ensuring correct justice
• Ensuring correct rituals
• Gaining knowledge of personal and world rhythms

Things to do
1. List in your runic journal the oaths that you have taken. Note whether you have kept them or not. How are you living up to these oaths? If any have been broken, what can you do to redress this?
2. Ride a horse. Think of the Raidho rune as you do so. Does this activity give you an increased understanding of the rune?

Thoughts to meditate upon
1. What am I most rational about?
2. When do I give the best advice?
3. What ideals do I stand up for?

Three ways to enact Raidho in your life
1. Take stock of your life. Are you living according to your ideals?
2. Fix any wrongs that you have caused to your friends and family.
3. Practice an exercise, art, or craft that involves rhythm—dance, sing, play an instrument. Alternatively, go and watch a live band, dance troupe, or something else that can inspire your sense of rhythm.

KENAZ

Name Kenaz—Torch

Alternative shapes

Number 6

Keywords Rune of all aspects of creativity.
The rune of shaping, skilled work, and artistry.

Rune poem stanzas

> K (Torch) is to every living person known by its fire
> it is clear and bright it usually burns
> when the noble-men rest inside the hall.
> OERP

> K (Sore) is the curse of children;
> grief makes a man pale.
> ONRP

> K (Sore) is the bale of children   and a scourge
>   and the house of rotten flesh.
> Whip.   "King"
> OIRP

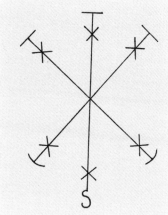

The Thief-Finder. A magical sign that reflects the sixfold pattern of Kenaz, from the *Galdrabók*. It is the sign "to find out a thief."

MEANING

Kenaz is the rune of creativity. Shape your skills and re-create your life. Kenaz is the torch—a sign of illumination, the bright light of self-knowledge, which is a major aim of the rune worker who follows Odin's path of the quest for knowledge. This light focuses on personal work and fosters individuality. It also helps bring our personal work and personal focus back into the world.

Kenaz is a sign of awakening, growth, willed shaping, and creation—the creative control of energy fire is a quintessential symbol of human achievement. Fire will be destructive if unchecked, but if controlled and disciplined, it may create beautiful and useful things.

Creativity raises humans to the level of the mysterious powers. The creative urge is the urge to shape the environment toward something different or to preserve it actively from destruction. The smith takes ore and fashions a sword or a ring. The cook takes leeks and potatoes and crafts a hearty soup. These things did not exist, except in the realm of ideas, before the creative urge and skill worked through the crafter.

The dissolution aspect of Kenaz is also very important to its meaning. To create a work of art, we destroy the paint and pristine canvas. To work with runes is to reshape the rune worker's objective world in some ways or, on the inner level, reshaping oneself.

A danger of the runes is that of uncontrolled subjectivity, which is warned of by the Kenaz rune. The "sore" of the rune poems exemplifies the swelling and creative urge—but in its negative aspect. Physical sores erupt when there is a bodily imbalance. The rune poems warn of the unwise or uninitiated use of the rune. Wrongful use of any of the runes may lead to dissolution or uncontrolled creation. Both are detrimental to the development of the rune worker. With no regard to external standards, the enthusiastic magician may be afflicted with the negative aspects of Kenaz—uncontrolled shaping. This sort of "mental sore" may be extremely unbalancing to the rune initiate and leave him or her in a maze of uncontrollable dimensions. Fortunately, the cure for this is easy—to "rest inside the hall," as the OERP suggests. If you do find yourself becoming unbalanced in any way, take a break. You could follow a nonesoteric hobby or catch up with your friends.

KENAZ EXERCISES

Galdra

Kenaz Kenaz Kenaz/KKKKKKKKK/Ke-Ke-Ke-Ke/Ka-Ka-Ka-Ka/Kenaz Kenaz Kenaz

Magical uses

- Creative inspiration
- Crafting
- Love magic

Things to do

This is the essential rune of crafts, so try any craft that catches your interest. There's plenty that you could try—basically any northern European craft. Here are some crafts that are relatively easy to access and do not require too many tools:

1. Try making a traditional food such as apple strudel or bread.
2. Try making some heathen tools for rituals, such as a drinking horn, wooden bowl, or fire pot.
3. Try making gifts yourself and encouraging heathen craftsmanship by giving them to friends and family.

Thoughts to meditate upon

- What are my most creative abilities?
- When am I most aware?
- How can I control my energy so that I become more aware or am aware for longer periods?

Three ways to enact Kenaz in your life

1. Learn a technical skill.
2. Learn an art.
3. Encourage creativity in your community—support local artists.

GEBO

Name Gebo—Gift
Number 7
Keywords The gift rune. Hospitality and sharing. Sacrifice and exchange of oaths.
Rune poem stanza

G (Gift) is for every man   a pride and praise,
help and worthiness;   (and) of every homeless adventurer,
it is estate and substance   for those who have nothing else.
OERP

MEANING

Gebo is the gift rune. Share what you know and your power will grow.

In the Germanic world, being hospitable was a great virtue. Wealth was measured by how generous you could be. Rulers were frequently referred to in *kennings* (poetic speech) as "givers of rings" and similar terms. Gifts can start and cement social connections. The noble who desired to lead an expedition was expected to be generous both before and after the hard work.

Accepting gifts could lead one into a state of unwanted dependence, as happened in the Anglo-Saxon tale of Beowulf. When confronted with the awesome beast Grendel, most of Beowulf's men fled, despite the fact that they owed their livelihood and their wealth to the hero.

Misers were thought to be lacking in social skills and perhaps corrupted by wealth.

Such is the fate of Fáfnir, the dragon who started out as a giant but was obsessed with his hoard—until the dragon slayer came along. In the Northern tradition, it was believed that wealth should be shared (see Fehu, pages 54–57).

In the lore, Gebo is the sacrifice of the self to one's fellows in times of need or to oneself when taking up the runes (see Ansuz, pages 66–69). Gebo is also the rune of the oath ring upon which great and binding bonds are sworn. The Ansuz rune symbolizes the substance of Odin's sacrifice and the Gift of Consciousness, while Gebo is the act of giving the gift.

The lore also warns about being too generous and about being too pushy with gifts, whether they be for gods or men:

It is unbidden
than to sacrifice too much;
a gift always looks for repayment.

Gebo is the force of exchange between two people or between a person and a group. One of the most important aspects of this is exchange between life partners. The gift of exchange between two partners brings much joy—see Wunjo, pages 82–85. One of the great dramatic scenes of the *Edda* is the Valkyrie, deep in magical sleep, being awoken by the heroic Sigurd (Siegfried in the German versions). This is not just a love story, but a retelling of the mysterious communion of the self with the runic aspects of the self.

The gift rune oversees the smooth running of all that requires exchange, hospitality, and interpersonal ethics. As such it is the ideal rune for steadfast rune-study groups.

GEBO EXERCISES

Galdra
Gebo Gebo Gebo
Ge-Ge-Ge-Ge
Go-Go-Go-Go
Gebo Gebo Gebo

Magical uses
• Gaining wisdom
• Making sexual magic
• Achieving family harmony

Things to do
1. Share something that you value.
2. Find or start a rune-study group in your community.

Thoughts to meditate upon
Use each of these questions as a focus for a meditation session. When the session is over, record in your runic journal the answers that emerged from the meditation.
1. What nonphysical gifts do I give to others?
2. In what ways am I hospitable?
3. What have I sacrificed in order to gain wisdom?

Three ways to enact Gebo in your life
1. Give a traditional gift, perhaps one you have made yourself.
2. Be hospitable. Give a housewarming gift or invite friends and family over for dinner.
3. Do something special and unexpected for your family.

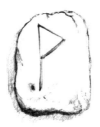

WUNJO

Name Wunjo—Joy

Alternative shape P D

Number 8

Keywords Rune of joy. Rune of harmony and holistic approaches to the self. Rune of well-being and social cohesion.

Rune poem stanza

W (Joy) is had   *by the one who knows few troubles*
pains and sorrows,   *and to him who himself has*
power and blessedness,   *and also the plenty of towns.*
OERP

MEANING

Wunjo is the rune of joy. Encourage joyfulness by engaging in worthwhile activities. Joy is the reward that comes when we are in a harmonious state. This can occur in many ways—we may have achieved a goal, fallen in love, or balanced our inner and outer lives. The joy rune can be sought in pleasures of both mind and body. The Northern tradition promotes the concept of the body as integrated with the sense of self, with no need to deny oneself (legal) desires when necessary.

Most people have life goals that involve an increase of happiness and a decrease in woes. These goals are encouraged in Ásatrú. The rune poem says that we should "know few troubles." In this modern age, alienation and stress are common realities. By seeking joy we can counter this malaise. Joy can come through giving and receiving gifts (see Gebo, pages 78–81). However, this rune teaches us that we cannot rely on others to make us happy. We have to strive for our own sense of joy. We also have to understand that people have different goals and perspectives. Then our lives and our interactions with others will be more fruitful.

One way to encourage our sense of the joyful is to enhance the happiness of those in our family or circle of friends. Bringing joy to the clan can come from doing something to make your family proud. This may take the form of hosting a family gathering for a significant life event (perhaps a coming of age, a marriage, or a naming ceremony), or even for something specialized such as sharing the results of your family history searches. Friends and family may even become interested in participating in rune study with you or in joining in some of the seasonal festivals of Ásatrú, such as Yule or Easter.

Well-being is linked to joy. The most stressed people always seem to be those with the least laughter. The Wunjo rune shows that having a sense of joy can help maintain your health. Joy can make you stronger.

WUNJO EXERCISES

Galdra
Wunjo Wunjo Wunjo
Wu-Wu-Wu-Wu
Wo-Wo-Wo-Wo
Wunjo Wunjo Wunjo

Magical uses
• Strengthening friendships
• Eliminating alienation
• Developing awareness of the multiplicity of human perspectives

Things to do
1. Organize a family event or a feast for your friends.
2. Have fun. Go out dancing.
3. Carve a bind rune for health.

Thoughts to meditate upon
Use each of these questions as a focus for a meditation session. When the session is over, record in your runic journal the answers that emerged from the meditation.
1. What are my greatest joys?
2. How do I share happiness?
3. Can I plan to achieve joy?

Three ways to enact Wunjo in your life
1. Make peace with your family. Resolve feuds over small misunderstandings.
2. Strengthen your friendships.
3. Celebrate after achieving a goal.

HAGALAZ

Name Hagalaz—Hail (stone)

Alternative shapes

Number 9

Keywords The hail rune. Crisis and sudden change, "storm and stress." The condensation of power.

Rune poem stanzas

> H (Hail) is the whitest of grains,   it comes from high in heaven.
> A shower of wind hurls it,   then it turns to water.
> OERP

> H (Hail) is the coldest of grains;
> Hropt shaped the world in ancient times.
> ONRP

> H (Hail) is a cold grain   and a shower of sleet
> and the bane of snakes.
> Hail.   "Battle-leader"
> OIRP

MEANING

Hagalaz is the rune of hail, storms, and crisis. Use it to reorganize your priorities. Hagalaz symbolizes potential power and the idea that transformation is not always positive. It can therefore be very destructive. Before you try to change anything, you should think carefully about the possible effects of your actions. When you can plan your actions in the correct way—through trial and error, applying common sense, and considering the traditional ways—you are well on your way to being wise.

Hagalaz can also be very protective. It can indicate that power can be deflected or harnessed. This rune can be used to ward the home or other holy places, acting as a shield.

This is also the rune of crisis. Hagalaz is the hailstone, the "white grain" that often heralds storms. A hailstorm can destroy a good harvest. Often, we cannot control negative situations when they are sprung upon us, but we can learn to think like strategists or battle leaders and use or transform negative situations to our advantage. At the very least, we can overcome them wisely.

Hagalaz is the meeting point of Cosmic Fire and Ice. The seed form and power of transformation, Hagalaz is considered to be the "mother rune"—from it the cosmic pattern of the rune row developed. This cosmic pattern can be related to the threefold pattern inherent in the Hagalaz rune and in the pattern of many of the other Northern symbols—such as the Yggdrasill cosmology (see Chapter Three)—and in the natural world, as in the three-line shape of the snowflake, for example.

Hagalaz is the ninth rune. Nine is the most sacred and magical number in the runic world. There are nine nights that Odin hangs on the World Tree, Nine Worlds on the Cosmic Tree, and many other significant symbols with this number. Being aware of the Nine Noble Virtues (see Chapter Eight) can give you a sense of completeness in the physical and metaphysical realms and can also be a good starting point for developing your own balanced sense of ethics.

The Hagalaz structure
in a snowflake

HAGALAZ EXERCISES

Galdra

Hagalaz Hagalaz Hagalaz/Ha-Ha-Ha-Ha/Haaaaaaaaa/Hagalaz Hagalaz Hagalaz

Magical uses

- Protection
- Balance
- Self-evolution—realizing your potential

Things to do

1. Learn self-defense. If you are already skilled at a form of self-defense, take up another activity in this field, such as a martial art.
2. Protect your home. Think about ways to do this. Join a neighborhood group, see the local police for ideas on securing your home, or investigate methods others have used.
3. Prepare for a negative situation. Think of this in mental and physical terms. For example, if there is a flood in your area, what should you do to prepare yourself and your family both emotionally and physically?

Thoughts to meditate upon

1. What has been the greatest crisis in my life?
2. How can I be prepared for catastrophe?
3. How can I use stress more creatively for my own purposes?

Three ways to enact Hagalaz in your life

1. Complete a project you have already started. First, outline for yourself the purpose of the project and then note down the steps you can take to achieve this.
2. Transform a situation from one that has not been working into one that is working.
3. Try to rid yourself of something negative—a habit, attitude, or other limiting behavior.

NAUTHIZ

Name Nauthiz—Need

Alternative shape †

Number 10

Keywords The rune of need. A resistance that leads to greater refinement and improved work. The rune of testing.

Rune poem stanzas

N (Need) is constricting on the chest,
although to the children of men it often becomes
a help and salvation nevertheless
if they head it in time.
OERP

N (Need) makes for a difficult situation;
the naked freeze in the frost.
ONRP

N (Need) is the grief of the bondmaid   and a hard condition
*   and toilsome work.*
Work.   "Descendant of the mist"
OIRP

MEANING

Nauthiz is the rune of need, that which drives us to great heights. Need is a friction that resists our actions. One aspect of need is the need-fire, that self-generated flame that can be created by rubbing two branches of wood together. A need-fire is used in an emergency—and for lighting the most sacred flames.

We all want certain things in life. Many of these goals have been placed in our minds by peer pressure, clever marketing, or our upbringing. In moments of crisis (Hagalaz, pages 86–89) or in intensely inspired moments (Ansuz, pages 66–69), we may get a clear picture of what we really need and the appropriate way to achieve this. Tremendous clarity and a strong sense of purpose are generated when we do what we need to do. However, if we are not prepared to do what we need to do—this requires hard work and much challenge—bad luck may result, as well as a sense of meaninglessness.

Nauthiz is the resistance we face with limited resources. We have to make the best out of whatever situation we are in. Having a limited focus often helps to bring forth great works. The rune worker may be forced to focus on one thing and master particular skills. When you focus on what you need, rather than what is fleeting or pleases others, you will have a much greater chance of success—in any field.

NAUTHIZ EXERCISES

Galdra

Nauthiz Nauthiz Nauthiz/Na-Na-Na-Na/Nu-Nu-Nu-Nu/Ni-Ni-Ni-Ni/Nauthiz Nauthiz Nauthiz

Magical uses

• Protection
• Divination
• Development of will

Things to do

1. Start a need-fire.
2. Make a list of what you need to do.

Thoughts to meditate upon

1. What ordeals have I faced?
2. What do I really need in life?
3. How can I better use my current resources?

Three ways to enact Nauthiz in your life

1. Take a few days to think about who you are, what you want to be, and what you need to do in life.
2. Create a list of what you think you need to do in your life.
3. Then strike off the needs you think have been put there by advertising, social convention, or the expectations of others—needs that are not truly your life goals. Start working now on the goals that remain.

ISA

Name Isa—Ice

Number 11

Keywords Rune of contraction, concentration, and stasis. Rune of stillness and silence.

Rune poem stanzas

> I (Ice) is very cold   and exceedingly slippery;
> it glistens, clear as glass,   very much like gems,
> a floor made of frost   is fair to see.
> OERP

> I (Ice), we call the broad bridge;
> the blind need to be led.
> ONRP

> I (Ice) is the rind of the river   and the roof of the waves
> and a danger for fey men.
> Ice.   "One who wears the boar helmet"
> OIRP

MEANING

Isa is the rune of concentration and stillness. The silence of the ice. This rune enables you to focus on particular tasks. Isa is the stasis that is beyond *Thurs* (sleep) and rest. With a conscious approach, reaching this state can prove a very enlightening experience. When everything else is set aside for the time, we are allowing our horizons to expand.

Ice is one of the essential "elemental" ingredients in the Northern cosmology. The flow of Ice from Niflheim meets the flow of Fire from Muspellheim and leads to the creation of the universe. The two polar extremes create a third condition that transcends the sum of the parts—for example, in the Northern realm, Fire + Ice = universe.

Ice is the contraction, the condensing into a potent unit of runic force, whereas its opposite is the expansive force (Fehu, pages 54–57). Isa is the rune of the contraction and stillness of ice. Isa is suited to all undertakings that require intense concentration. In the Rune Gild theory of the ninefold soul lore (see Chapter Three), it is the force of Isa that bonds the various parts together. It is in the winterlike conditions symbolized by Isa—stillness, silence, and darkness—that we can best focus on inner work.

The "broad bridge" of ice mentioned in the *Old Norse Rune Poem* probably represents the line formed by this rune. All runes are angular and thus are made from lines. Through the use of these angled lines, we may form a bridge with which we can connect to the other worlds of Yggdrasill. This bridge may refer to the practice of meditation on a single rune.

As with all runes, Isa does carry dangers and the icy path is easy to slip on. Isa demonstrates that overuse can lead to stasis—a freezing of development. Too much focus on using Isa for self-exploration can lead to negative, egocentric behavior; Fehu or Gebo are good icebreakers for this.

ISA EXERCISES

Galdra Isa Isa Isa/Iiiiiiiiii/Issssssssss/Iiiiiiiiii/Isa Isa Isa

Magical uses
• Development of concentration
• Psychological integration

Things to do
1. Try ice-skating, skiing, or another winter sport. What special skills do you need for dealing with ice and snow that are not tested in any other way?
2. Meditate on Isa. Along with Fehu, it is a very good choice for a rune with which to start meditation. It highlights the polar nature of rune work.

Isa meditation
This is a very relaxing meditation and is helpful before any runic work.

Use the Breathing Exercise outlined in Chapter Two (page 26). Start controlling your breathing. As you fall into the rhythm of regular breathing, visualize the Isa stave in front of you, slowly contracting to a thin line. Imagine it eventually becoming so thin that you cannot see it. Then focus your concentration inward into a single point. At this moment, become aware that you are in a place void of motion, sound, and time.

Three ways to enact Isa in your life
1. Cultivate stillness and silence as a personal retreat.
2. Recognize that resistance is useful—anything worthwhile should be a challenge. Use the challenge to encourage yourself to strive for the best.
3. Recognize the negative aspects of runes. Note that when the forces in our lives—however positive—are too great, blocked, or used inappropriately, there will be negative results.

JERA

Name Jera—Year, harvest

Alternative shapes

Number 12

Keywords Rune of the good harvest, of the right use of natural/organic processes. Rune of results and rewards. The fruit of the well-planted tree.

Rune poem stanzas

J (Harvest) is the hope of men, when god lets,
holy king of heaven,   the Earth give
her bright fruits   to the nobles and the needy.
OERP

J (Harvest) is the profit of all men;
I say that Frodhi was generous.
ONRP

J (Harvest) is the profit of all men   and a good summer
and a ripened field.
Year.   "All-ruler"
OIRP

MEANING

Jera is the rune of the cycle of the year. You are rewarded with a good harvest if you understand and use wisely the cycles of the natural world. In the early runic era, this would have been understood mainly as the agricultural cycles. These were celebrated by many of the cultural and religious festivals.

The Jera rune symbolizes in particular the hard work and great reward of the harvest. Right work bears good fruits. Harvest only occurs if you have sown your seeds correctly, taking into account the timing and environmental factors. As the Icelandic proverb says: "A sitting crow goes hungry."

Harvest also requires a great deal of teamwork, so it is a good time to set aside petty differences so that all may benefit. Harvest is also a time to pitch in and help your kin and friends. A well-earned feast is the result.

Of course, this "harvest" is not only the literal harvest of crops. As with all of the runes, there are a multiplicity of meanings, from the natural cycles to numinous experiences of the higher self. The harvest represents an eternal return of the cycles of nature and the human and divine worlds. Seeds are sown, reaped, and next season planted again.

The "generous god" mentioned in the rune poems is Freyr, the Lord of the World. Freyr is the god of harvests, peace, prosperity, and pleasure. Freyr is the most important of the Vanir tribe of gods, a popular deity associated with fertility.

It may seem strange to read today that the Germanic tribes and Viking folk actually wanted peace. In fact they were no more bloodthirsty than other peoples of the same age, and the reason for much of the fighting was to win their fortune so that they could afford to settle down and raise their families.

Jera promotes Frith—peace. This occurs when society is functioning well and according to law and ethics. In the tradition, Frith is not a static peace without friction, as some struggle is always required for growth, but rather an absence of needless war.

The god Freyr

JERA EXERCISES

Galdra

Jera Jera Jera/Je-Je-Je-Je/Ja-Ja-Ja-Ja/Jera Jera Jera

Magical uses

- Achieving peace and harmony
- Increasing creativity
- Enhancing fertility

Things to do

1. Plant a tree. The best trees to plant would be native to your area to encourage native animals to your home or fruit trees to provide you with a growing (and nutritious) example of Jera.
2. Grow your own herbs and vegetables using organic methods. Your cooking skills will improve if you have fresh herbs on hand, and organic vegetables will nourish your family.
3. Hold a harvest feast and give place of honor to your own cooking and produce.

Thoughts to meditate upon

1. What does "harvest" mean for me?
2. How could I time the events in my life better? How would this improve my life?
3. How can I encourage Frith (peace) in my life?

Three ways to enact Jera in your life

1. Write down a list of the cycles that affect you.
2. Think about these for a few days and then list some suggestions for using them more wisely. For example, if winter rain makes you miserable, think of ways to make the experience of having to stay inside more enjoyable.
3. Make Frith (peace) with someone with whom you have had a disagreement.

IHWAZ

Name Ihwaz—Yew (tree)

Number 13

Keywords Axis of enlightenment. The process of becoming. Traveling through the World Tree.

Rune poem stanzas

> EI (Yew) is, on the outside,   a rough tree
> and hard, firm in the earth,   keeper of the fire,
> supported by roots,   (it is a) joy on the estate.
> OERP

> Y (Yew) is the greenest wood in the winter;
> there is usually, when it burns, singeing.
> ONRP

> Y (Yew) is a strung bow   and brittle iron
> and a giant of the arrow.
> Bow.   "Descendant of Yngvi"
> OIRP

MEANING

The yew rune increases personal power and discipline. Use it to climb the World Tree.

The yew tree was one of the main sacred trees of the Northern world. It is an extremely long-living tree, and there are many yew trees in Europe that probably have lived to see the suppression, hiding, and rebirth of the heathen religions—especially since many of them still stand in graveyards and churchyards, which were built on top of heathen sacred places.

Yew wood is excellent for making bows, as it is flexible and very strong. In this capacity it may be associated with the god Ullr, who is famed for his prowess in archery and skiing. Ullr is also the god to call upon in duels. These are all skills that test personal limits.

Ihwaz is the rune of the vertical climb along the World Tree (see Chapter Three). It is the cosmic axis, the vertical trunk—the path of communication between extremes, between the higher and lower worlds along the World Tree.

The World Tree links the realms of consciousness (Asgard) and those of humanity (Midgard) with that of death (Hel). Because of this, Ihwaz can be used to examine our thoughts on death and test them against the Northern tradition.

The fire referred to in the rune poems is that of the self-kindled fire, which has been

generated by Nauthiz and may be harnessed by Kenaz. Through this internal flame, many hidden strengths may be drawn out and inner goals realized.

It is also useful to look at alternative representations of this rune in later systems. In the Younger Futhark tradition, the yew rune is sometimes called the "death rune," mainly because it mediates between life and death. In the

The death rune

Younger Futhark rune row, it is the inversion of the Elder Elhaz or "life rune." However, this idea of death is not final, as it involves a journey into another state of being or possible rebirth into one's ancestral line.

In medieval times, Ihwaz was the forbidding symbol of the *Wolfsangle* or "Wolf's hook." This rune is still used in the heraldic shields of several towns in Germany. It graphically displays the concept of passing into a different

Wolfsangle or Wolf's hook

state of being and arising again—a process of seeking the experience and synthesis of opposites.

IHWAZ EXERCISES

Galdra Ihwaz Ihwaz Ihwaz/EI.../EI.../Ihwaz Ihwaz Ihwaz

Magical uses
• Understanding Yggdrasill
• Realization of life/death mysteries
• Increase of personal power

Things to do
1. Try archery.
2. Combat gossip in your everyday life and in the world of rune workers.
3. Be disciplined about a task you need to do. Avoid jumping from one thing to the next. For example, if you need to get your finances together, stop planning for a vacation.

Thoughts to meditate upon
Use each of these questions as a focus for a meditation session. When the session is over, record in your runic journal the answers that emerged from the meditation.
1. What extremes have I experienced?
2. How do I see the role of death in life?
3. What is the limit of my personal power?

Three ways to enact Ihwaz in your life
1. Think about the worlds on Yggdrasill. What are the differences between Asgard, Hel, and Midgard? What can knowledge of these worlds do for you?
2. Why would someone want to climb the World Tree?
3. What do you think about death? How has death affected you in the past, and what is your idea of what will happen to you when you die?

PERTHRO

Name Perthro—Lot Box

Alternative shapes

Number 14

Keywords Rune of change, synchronicity (meaningful coincidences), cause and effect, and chance. This is the rune of rune casting and of the threefold processes of arising, becoming, and arising anew (as in the birth/life, death, and rebirth cycle).

Rune poem stanza

> P (Lot Box) is always
> among bold men,
> in the beer hall,
> OERP

> play and laughter
> where the warriors sit
> happy together.

MEANING

Perthro is the lot box, the container of rune staves in divination or of dice in any test of your luck. The shape of the rune is suggestive of a well—the Well of Wyrd. From the prose *Edda*, this holy well is described in *Gylfaginnung 14*:

> *There a beautiful hall stands beneath the ash by the well, and from that hall come three maidens, they who are so called: Urdhr, Verdhandi, Skuld. These maidens shape the lives of men. We call them Norns.*

The three Norns are sisters, who shape our fates (Old English *wyrd*). They are thought to be continually weaving the fates of all beings. The three Norns are called Urdhr (that which has become), Verdhandi (that which is becoming) and Skuld (that which shall be). These are roughly equivalent to the "past," "present," and "future" respectively, but these concepts are far more dynamic and interconnected in the runic worldview than they are in our own.

Perthro combines the idea of cause and effect (the way things occur on the natural level) with the theory of synchronicity—when we have "meaningful happenings" (for example, when we are thinking of a friend and he or she calls us on the phone). This is a potent feature of rune work and many people, as they learn the runes, become aware that many seemingly random acts around them are in actual fact meaningful.

The concept of Wyrd has been assumed to be a fatalistic concept in Germanic thought, but it is not a form of predestination. The difference is that past and present actions are assumed to affect the future in certain ways. Through experience, wisdom, and rune reading, the rune caster may trace back these threads of fate to find reasons for current occurrences and to map possible future trends and problems in a person's life. In the *Edda*, Odin learns that he is going to be killed by the Fenris Wolf and that the World Tree will be destroyed at **Ragnarök**. The knowledge of this is the first step toward changing fate—toward controlling destiny.

Like the related idea of karma, one's Wyrd is also influenced along ancestral lines. While there is no moralistic understanding or underpinning of Wyrd in the Northern tradition as there is in Indian karma, there is the belief that the Wyrd does have ancestral roots and this is an additional factor to consider when consciously deciding to alter our path.

Perthro is the rune of rune divination (see Chapter Five). Rune divination is much more than mere fortune telling for entertainment. It is about understanding our Wyrd from a holistic, hyperconscious perspective—think of the intense gaze of Odin. It is no coincidence that the Well of Wyrd is related to Mimir's Well, where Odin has hidden (sacrificed) an eye for knowledge of his inner world and ours.

PERTHRO EXERCISES

Galdra

Perthro Perthro Perthro/Pe-Pe-Pe-Pe/Po-Po-Po-Po/Perthro Perthro Perthro

Magical uses
- Perception of wyrd
- Divination

Things to do
1. Find a natural spring in your area. If it is quiet enough, meditate there and think of Perthro.
2. Play dice games (although gambling is not recommended). There are plenty of skill and luck dice games that you could play with friends. Visit your local hobby store or find a book on games in the library.

Thoughts to meditate upon
1. How can I test myself in the world so that I add more constructive challenges to my life?
2. What "games" do I play with others—some useful and fun, some for other purposes? Why? How can I learn to modify some of these for better ends?
3. What is my Wyrd?

Three ways to enact Perthro in your life
1. Become a rune caster. Explore and gain proficiency with rune divination (see Chapter Five).
2. Test your luck. Go outside of your comfort zone and achieve something worthwhile. When did you last venture outside this zone? What did you do? How did you feel?
3. Think about where your path in life is taking you. Is it going where you like or need it to go? What would you have to alter in order for you to get to where you need to be (see Nauthiz, pages 90–93)?

ELHAZ

Name Elhaz—Elk

Alternative shapes

Number 15

Keywords Rune of communication with, and perception of, divine and mythic states. Also the rune of the dangers inherent in such an undertaking.

Rune poem stanza

> Z (Elk's) sedge has its home   *most often in the fen,*
> *it waxes in the water*   *and grimly wounds,*
> *and burns with blood*   *any bairn*
> *who in any way*   *tries to grasp it.*
> OERP

MEANING

Elhaz is the rune of your luck and guardian spirits. This rune is the mystery of the communication between the human and his or her higher "divine" self. It acts as a tutelary being or guardian spirit, as in the *Hamingja* concept (see Chapter Three) in the runic psychology model. Guardian spirits like this often take the form of an animal. Elhaz is also associated with protective beings such as the Valkyries, those warrior maidens who are the "Choosers of the Slain" on battlefields and take the brave dead to their halls in Asgard.

Communicating with one's higher self or guardian spirits can be dangerous. It can lead to imbalance if attempted by the unready or for the wrong reasons, such as escaping from the real world. This is the reason for the warnings of the rune poem.

The shape of the rune itself is associated with numinous powers. It resembles the open-handed gesture for offering help and the arm position for prayer or for calling on the sacred in the Germanic religious traditions. (This position is also used in modern Ásatrú rites.)

The elk is a sacred animal. In the archaic forms of Germanic religious tradition, there were twin elk gods called Alcis. Their divine prototypes inhabited the World Tree, nibbling at leaves and bark. The elk is also associated with the god Freyr, who is armed at the great battle of Ragnarök with a horn from a deer.

The protective aspects of Elhaz are evident in another association—with the Valkyries. These beings often travel in swan form, which, when flying, resembles the shape of the Elhaz rune. This is another connection with the idea of the

Hamingja in its shape-shifting aspect. The connection between swans and magical/religious warrior women is not made only in the Elder lore. More modern folklore has carried this interesting concept to us in the form of the *Wilis*, those deathly spirit women we know from the ballet of *Swan Lake*.

Elhaz is the rune of the protective god Heimdall. With his resounding horn of alarm and keen eyes and ears he keeps watch over the Bifrost bridge of the Northern mythic world—the connection between the Nine Worlds.

Holy elk with Elhaz rune

112

ELHAZ EXERCISES

Galdra
Elhaz Elhaz Elhaz/ZZZZZZZZZ/Ze-Ze-Ze-Ze/Za-Za-Za-Za/Elhaz Elhaz Elhaz

Magical uses
• Protection
• Communication with gods and other mythological creatures
• Luck

Things to do
1. Go animal watching. If you can, watch some animals that have ties to old heathen myths, such as swans, elk, deer, goats, and ravens.
2. Keep watch on something that affects our freedom, such as attacks on freedom of religion.

Thoughts to meditate upon
1. What animals do I feel inspired by? Why?
2. What are some of the dangers of the runes? How can I counter these dangers?
3. What Northern gods/goddesses interest me? Why?

Three ways to enact Elhaz in your life
1. Acquaint yourself with local rune-working groups. Local community centers, esoteric bookstores, or the Internet should help. Many groups have open events you can participate in with no commitment.
2. Search for your "animal guardian." The wilderness is the best place to seek, but you can visit a zoo or a farm also. Note to which animals you are drawn.
3. Listen to your inner guidance. Cultivate your intuition and your inner guides. These give us much advice—if only we will listen.

SOWILO

Name Sowilo—Sun

Alternative shapes

Number 16

Keywords Rune of the sun, rune of individual victory, good guidance, and honor.

Rune poem stanzas

> S (Sun) is by sea-men   always hoped for
> when they fare far away   over the fishes bath [sea],
> until the brine-stallion [ship] they bring to land.
> OERP

> S (Sun) is the light of the lands;
> I bow to the doom of holiness.
> ONRP

> S (Sun) is the shield of the clouds   and a shining glory
> and the life-long sorrow of ice.
> Wheel.   "Descendant of the victorious one"
> OIRP

MEANING

Sowilo is the rune of the goal and the individual will that is needed to reach that goal. It is the rune of the light of the sun, of good guidance, and of acting with honor. The sun is a potent symbol. We are all dependent on it for survival, life, and growth. The rune poems give a beautiful interpretation of the sun, a combination of literal, poetic, and mythic aspects.

The rune system is multifaceted. While the runes are numinous concepts, their forms are often expressed in very active work in Midgard. Sowilo, with its goal-oriented nature, is one such rune. It teaches us that it is not enough to understand any rune on an intellectual level only. To be fully brought into consciousness, the runes need to be experienced and applied.

Sowilo may help us to refine goals by focusing us on the journey that lies ahead. In the world of spiritual seeking, people will often come to some plateau and believe that they are at the end of the path. But the path goes ever onward. The plateau is not the end of the line—it is a step only.

Sowilo is the necessary guidance (even if from within) that we need before undertaking any difficult journey or personal quest. The sun itself was thought to be personified in the figure of Sol, perhaps connected to the goddess Freyja, who, as Syr, was the golden sow of the sun. The sun was considered a symbol of religious significance and is shown by the symbol of the Trundholm chariot, which is a representation of a sacred horse pulling a great sun disk on a chariot across the sky.

Another special sign associated with Sowilo is that of the **sun wheel**, in its solid or whirling forms. This dynamic sign is that of the accumulation of power and indicates the wheels by which the "chariot" of Sowilo undertakes its procession, as well as the guiding beacon that draws wayfarers home. The zigzag shape of this rune is also the path of the serpent, an animal of Odin, who is able to win knowledge and wisdom through delving into dark and hidden places. It is the rune of gaining inspiration through seeking the mysterious.

Sun disk

SOWILO EXERCISES

Galdra

Sowilo Sowilo Sowilo/SSSSSSSSS/So-So-So-So/Si-Si-Si-Si/Sowilo Sowilo Sowilo

Magical uses

• Individual success
• Asserting the will
• Learning the paths and centers of the Nine Worlds

Things to do

1. Participate in navigating or orienteering.
2. List three of your goals. How far have you come in achieving them? Will these goals help to improve your life? Reword them now if they do not do so and you are not making much progress with them.
3. Give guidance—give good advice to friends and family when you can.

Thoughts to meditate upon

1. Where should I seek guidance?
2. What victories have I had in the past year?
3. Where should I travel next?

Three ways to enact Sowilo in your life

1. Promote solar energy.
2. Seek something mysterious. Find out about something obscure or hidden that has sparked your interest. For example, trace the origins of particular themes in myths and symbols.
3. Ask for and give feedback to your friends and contacts. Ask them if you are a good communicator, a generous person, etc. With honest feedback we can grow better.

TIWAZ

Name Tiwaz—The god Tyr

Alternative shape ᛏ

Number 17

Keywords Rune of balance, self-sacrifice, being true, faithfulness. Rune of victory.

Rune poem stanzas

T (Tyr) is a token,   it keeps troth well
with noble-men   always on its course
over the mists of night,   it never fails.
OERP

T (Tyr) is the one-handed among the Æsir;
the smith has to blow often.
ONRP

T (Tyr) is the one-handed god   and the leavings of the wolf
and the ruler of the temple.
Mars.   "Director"
OIRP

MEANING

Tiwaz represents analytical and logical thought and is good to call upon in any situation demanding levelheadedness and the ability to decide upon the correct action. This rune is named after Tyr, the god of the sky, war, and legal assemblies.

Tiwaz is described in the *OERP* as the pole star, the axis around which everything revolves and a reliable light for navigators to use to find their way home. Tiwaz is connected with the Germanic **Irminsûl** column, which is a symbol of victory, separation of earth and sky, and cosmic order. This idea is similar and connected to that of the Yggdrasill, the World Tree.

The Tyr rune promotes just conduct and victory for the just in any battle. Tyr is not a god of war for war's sake. The victory Tyr promotes is not that of the individual, but of victory for the whole, whether it be clan, tribe, or nation.

In rune magic, Tyr is known as a victory rune. In the *Sigdrífumál*, stanza 7, the Valkyrie tells the hero:

Victory-runes you should know,
if you would have victory,
and carve on the sword's hilt,
some on the groove-ridge,
some on the sword-rope,
and name Tyr twice
SIGDRÍFUMÁL, STANZA 7

Tiwaz is the rune of troth. Troth is about being true to yourself, your ideals, your gods, and your ancestors. The bonds between these and the self are tested in adversity. This is the rune of the keeping of oaths.

In the *OERP*, Tyr is named as the "Director of the Temple." In this role, Tiwaz is a good rune for those who are running or thinking of founding rune-study groups, or even running any sort of group, sacred or secular.

TIWAZ EXERCISES

Galdra

Tiwaz Tiwaz Tiwaz/Ti-Ti-Ti-Ti/Ta-Ta-Ta-Ta/Tiwaz Tiwaz Tiwaz

Magical uses

- Victory for the just
- Keeping the Troth

Things to do

1. Carve "victory runes" on your tools of trade or ceremonial knife.
2. A good inscription would be:

ᛋᛁᚷᛏᚤᚱ ᛋᛁᚷᛏᛁᚹᚨᛉ ᛏᛏ

Sig-Tyr inscription: Sig-Tyr, Sig-Tiwaz, TT
3. Think about your ideas on ethics. Do you think they are logical and well thought out? Test them with your friends in a friendly situation.

Thoughts to meditate upon

1. Am I true to my beliefs? Am I ethical?
2. What does Tyr mean to me?

Three ways to enact Tiwaz in your life

1. Make an oath and keep it. Oath keeping can be hard, especially when your oath is a very serious one.
2. Stand up for your rights—have your say.
3. Sacrifice something of value to help the well-being of all. For example, give up a weekend to help protect a local forest from destruction.

BERKANO

Name Berkano—Birch (goddess)

Alternative shapes ᛒ ᛒ ᛒ

Number 18

Keywords Rune of release and liberation of energy. Rune of birth and rebirth, rune of becoming. Rune of the mysteries of the birch goddess.

Rune poem stanzas

B (Birch) is without fruit
limbs without seed;
high on its crown
loaded with leaves,
OERP

but just the same it bears
it has beautiful branches
it is finely covered
touching the sky.

B (Birch-twig) is the limb greenest with leaves;
Loki brought the luck of deceit.
ONRP

B (Birch-twig) is a leafy limb   and a little tree
and a youthful wood.
Silver fir.   "Protector"
OIRP

MEANING

The birch rune is the releasing of energy, especially from that in seed form (see Ingwaz, pages 138–141). The seed can be that planted from what has been saved from last year's harvest (see Jera, pages 98–101), or a "seed" of a numinous substance, such as an idea. The Elder Troth has survived for so long not because there has been an unbroken tradition that can be traced back to the mysterious Elder rune masters, but because the runes themselves are planted in the two streams of culture and ancestry, and this has assured their survival.

Berkano is the passage from one state of being to the next, the moment of becoming or initiation. Because of this, it is the rune of major turning points, of the major rites of passage of birth, adolescence, marriage, and death. It is also the rune of the renewal of this process with each generation. In addition, Berkano presides over the idea of ancestral rebirth, whereby our deceased kin are reborn back into our families (see Othala, pages 146–149).

In the realm of the gods, Berkano is associated with the great goddess of the North, Freyja. Freyja is described in the prose *Edda* as:

And Freyja is the most glorious of the goddesses. She owns that dwelling in heaven which is called Fólkvangr, and wherever she rides to battle, then she owns half the slain…
And when she travels then she yokes two cats and sits in a chariot. She is the most favorable for men to invoke…
Love-songs well please her. It is good to invoke her for love.
GYLFAGINNUNG, 23–24

Berkano rules over transformational enclosures—sanctuaries, earth grottoes, caves or secluded groves, places where individuals retreat to undergo enlightenment. It protects the enclosures before they are broken open and the transformed individual returns to the world.

BERKANO EXERCISES

Galdra
Berkano Berkano Berkano/Be-Be-Be-Be/Ba-Ba-Ba-Ba/Bo-Bo-Bo-Bo/Berkano Berkano Berkano

Magical uses
• Rebirth
• Ensuring secrecy
• Bringing ideas to fruition

Things to do
1. Research the Northern goddesses. Make notes on those you find interesting or compelling.
2. Arrange a rite of passage for a family member or friend. These have often been secularized as birthday parties, baby showers, and the like, but they are also ways you can bring the influence of the runes to your family and circle of friends.

Thoughts to meditate upon
1. What Northern goddesses appeal to me? Why?
2. What ideas have I brought into being recently? What has happened with them?
3. What should I complete in my life?

Three ways to enact Berkano in your life
1. Plant seeds.
2. Visit a cave system. Find out about legends associated with the caves.
3. Visit a sanctuary or grove that you find inspiring. Spend some time there in contemplation.

EHWAZ

Name Ehwaz—Horse

Alternative shape ⊓
Number 19
Keywords Rune of teamwork and partnership. Rune of working together for common goals. Trust.
Rune poem stanza

> E (Horse) is, in front of the warriors,   the joy of noble-men,
> a charger proud on its hooves;   when concerning it, heroes—
> wealthy men—on war horses   exchange speech,
> and it is always a comfort   to the restless.
> OERP

MEANING

The horse rune encourages trust and teamwork. The most famous horse in the Germanic tradition is Odin's stead, Sleipnir. Sleipnir shares many adventures with the far-faring Odin. He could be considered a "divine horse," as he is the son of Loki (Loki had transformed himself into a mare). Sleipnir is able to ride farther and faster than any other horse, as well as over sea and air, and even all the way down to Hel. Sleipnir is considered the best of all horses and he also has eight legs. This is an ideal team relationship.

The horse was the prized animal companion of noblemen, as detailed in the *OERP*: it is described as the "joy of noble-men" and a comfort to those who get restless. Horses were always prized by the Indo-European peoples, the first to tame them, as they extended the ability to travel and expand the horizons of the known. The horse is also a figure of strength and fertility, dedicated to Freyr.

In heathen England, the idea of the divine horse was developed into twin divine ancestors called Hengist and Hersa (both horse-related names). In much later times in England this veneration of horses found something of a revival in the secretive fraternity called the Horseman's Word, a brotherhood of horse-whisperers—these are the people who, with special words and much empathy, put horses to ease.

Horses are still prized as companions by many, and there are many breeds, such as the Icelandic horse, that have direct links to the old heathen era. The horse was considered to be powerful in the later Icelandic *Galdrabók* traditions (see Chapter Six), and one of the Helms of Awe from that tradition is called *Ginnfaxi*—"Holy Mane."

The horse rune is symbolic of the *Fylgja*, or fetch. This is the doppelgänger often projected by someone who is dreaming or, in the rune system, traveling through the Nine Worlds. As well as being active in soul travel, the Ehwaz rune connects us to our higher principles and ideal self.

The horse rune promotes trust between two different entities and allows for teamwork and sharing. It is an ideal rune for any partnership and is suitable to use in any situation that requires trust, loyalty, and adhering to principles.

An Icelandic proverb reflects this wisdom: "Two is an army against one."

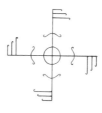

Ginnfaxi

EHWAZ EXERCISES

Galdra

Ehwaz Ehwaz Ehwaz/EEEEEEEEE/Eh-Eh-Eh-Eh/EEEEEEEEE/Ehwaz Ehwaz Ehwaz

Magical uses

• Developing trust and loyalty
• Soul travel

Things to do

1. Ride a horse.
2. Collaborate with another on a team project.
3. Research and practice lucid dreaming.

Thoughts to meditate upon

1. Who is part of my team?
2. Who are my peers?
3. How can I gain more allies?

Three ways to enact Ehwaz in your life

1. Visit someone who is extremely good with animals. Watch and learn how this person acts with the animals. If you are good with animals, teach someone else how to be at ease with them.
2. Write a list of the people that you trust. Think about why you trust them and note this down.
3. Reinforce your bonds with those whom you trust.

MANNAZ

Name Mannaz—Man, humanity

Alternative shape

Number 20

Keywords Rune of awareness. Rune of the link of the human soul and psyche with the realm of the gods and archetypes. The potential of each person.

Rune poem stanzas

M (Man) is in his mirth   dear to his kinsmen;
although each shall   depart from the other;
for the lord wants to commit,   by his decree,
that frail flesh   to the earth.
OERP

M (Man) is the increase of dust;
mighty is the talon-span of the hawk.
ONRP

M (Man) is the joy of man   and the increase of dust
and the adornment of ships.
Human.   "Generous one"
OIRP

MEANING

Mannaz is the rune of humanity. It celebrates the potential that is in each person and, as the rune poems show, especially those aspects that we can communicate to each other, such as our wisdom, wit, and works. Mannaz is the joyful experience of being human in Midgard and also a rune that can be grasped as a strong stave to depend on to give meaning to our lives.

Mannaz is also the rune of the whole, perfected person—the rune master. Having undergone various trials and tests, the master is expected to share his or her knowledge with those who follow the path.

At the same time, as this rune shows, initiation never ends—the path is the destination. The more we know of the runes—and of anything else worth knowing—the more we become aware of even larger horizons. This can be a frightening experience for the unprepared, but is cultivated by true seekers of the mysteries.

Mannaz is associated with the journey of the heroic warrior beyond death, the hall of Valhalla, the hall over which Odin presides. Most brave warriors dwell in either Folkvang—Freyja's Hall—or Valhalla. Here they continue to test themselves until they are needed to help the gods in the battle at Ragnarök.

A formula associated with Mannaz is *trua á matt ok megin*: "Trusting in one's own might and main." It shows that many heathens did not think the gods would have to do their work for them.

Mannaz is the rune of increasing mental powers in any capacity, such as learning new skills, increasing memory, and further disciplining one's thought in a myriad of ways, from meditation to magic.

MANNAZ EXERCISES

Galdra

Mannaz Mannaz Mannaz/MMMMMMMMM/Ma-Ma-Ma-Ma/Mannaz Mannaz Mannaz

Magical uses

- Increase in all mental powers
- Realizing the divine spark within

Things to do

1. Celebrate famous ancestors whom you respect. Write about them. Make a family tree. Discuss them with your family.
2. Expand your horizons—study something deeply.
3. Be self-reliant. Live by your own means and try to overcome problems on your own before seeking help.

Thoughts to meditate upon

1. How do I strive to be the best I can be?
2. How can I be more self-reliant?
3. What is my path?

Three ways to enact Mannaz in your life

1. Be self-reliant.
2. Learn to do something as well as you are able.
3. Seek to increase your knowledge, memory, and other faculties.

Write notes in your runic journal about occasions on which you have managed to achieve these three goals.

LAGUZ

Name Laguz—Lake, leek

Alternative shape ⌐

Number 21

Keywords Rune of the wider context of our becoming. Rune of acceptance of the challenges into which we are born. Rune of vital and protective growth.

Rune poem stanzas

L (Water) is to people seemingly unending,
if they should venture out   on an unsteady ship,
and the sea waves   frighten them very much,
and the brine-stallion   does not heed its bridle.
OERP

L (Water) is that which falls from the mountain
as a force; but gold (objects) are costly things.
ONRP

L (Water) is a churning lake   and a wide kettle
and the land of fish.
Lake.   "Praise-worthy one"
OIRP

135

MEANING

Laguz is the ancient waters from which organic life and energy spring. The OERP refers to Laguz as "seemingly unending." This could be interpreted as the world that each of us lives in, which gives us a context for all of our actions. We cannot choose when and where we are born—these are external factors to which we must adapt. The lake or leek rune enables you to grow in vital ways. Use it to guide and heal yourself in difficult situations.

Laguz can also indicate unstable or uncomfortable situations with which we should persevere in order to make ourselves stronger. These could include difficult social situations, standing up for our beliefs, or even trying to defuse conflict among friends.

Laguz is associated with holy wells, waterfalls, and sprinkling with water when a child is named in the ceremony known as *vatni ausa*, the heathen equivalent of the later act of baptism by Christians. The water from some wells was considered holy all over northern Europe. The prototype for these holy wells is the Well of Wyrd (see Perthro, pages 106–109). From this the Norns draw up holy water to help them know the fate of all things.

Wells and lakes were often places where sacrifices were left. Odin sacrifices one of his eyes into Mimir's Well (the Well of Wisdom), which is probably the Well of Wyrd. With Odin's eye in the Well of Wisdom, he can continually draw on the wisdom of all of the worlds.

The idea of gold (Fehu, see pages 54–57) being found in or near waters, possibly with some cost to the individual, is reminiscent of the treasures in other Old Germanic tales, such as the *Nibelung*. This could relate to the fact that many golden objects were offered to the gods by being deposited in water. The aspect of Freyja called *Gullveig* (gold intoxication), who is burned thrice but keeps returning, may be related. In psychological terms, from the depths (the unconscious), elements are raised and refined, though at some cost.

As the rune of the life force, Laguz is also known by its alternative name, *Laukuz*—the leek. This protective and holy plant has antiseptic and stimulant benefits. The leek rune enhances health on all levels and especially encourages the alternative medicine system of the North—herbalism, the practice of which has been unbroken since heathen times. Germanic records of herbalism survive in Anglo-Saxon charms.

LAGUZ EXERCISES

Galdra

Laguz Laguz Laguz/La-La-La-La/Lu-Lu-Lu-Lu/Laguz Laguz Laguz

Magical uses

- Guidance through initiatory tests
- Increase in vitality and life force

Things to do

1. Go swimming or sailing.
2. Prepare an herbal remedy.
3. Cook with a leek.

Thoughts to meditate upon

1. What does life mean to me?
2. What are the many "worlds" I inhabit?
3. How can I increase my life force?

Three ways to enact Laguz in your life

1. Use a wishing well.
2. Evaluate your health. Write a list of any ailments you have. Also, write a list of any ailments that your parents have that you may be predisposed to. How would you address all of these problems?
3. Challenge yourself—do something (legal) that is out of character for you. For example, seek out activities you would usually be afraid of—go mountain climbing or study a subject about which you know very little.

INGWAZ

Name Ingwaz—The god Ing

Alternative shapes

Number 22

Keywords Rune of isolation and separation, in order to grow at one's own pace. Rune of gestation and hidden mysteries. Rune of the storing of energy.

Rune poem stanza

ING was first   among the East-Danes
seen by men,   until he again eastward
went over the wave;   the wain followed on;
this is what the warriors   called the hero.
OERP

MEANING

The rune of gestation and internal growth, Ingwaz turns your focus inward. Make time for separation and introspection so that you can transform. The rune is shaped like an enclosed space—a womb, seed, or cave. It is the separation that is needed for any initiatory rites or processes, as the place where transformation occurs needs to be private. This separation is much like the chrysalis that a caterpillar needs in order to transform.

The process of separation and isolation is part of the magical tradition of the North.

Odin's rune winning occurs up a tree on nine windy nights (usually not a time when other people would be around), and the practice of *Utiseta*—"sitting out"—is a more shamanic technique ascribed to the *Seidhr* school of Northern magic, but has similarities with the Ingwaz rune. By sitting out, we can access the numinous realms and bring the wisdom back to the people or to our everyday lives.

It can be hard to separate from what is safe and known. However, the rune worker must learn that the mysteries often lead us to unexpected paths; though these are not physically dangerous, they do have pitfalls for the unwary. As Ingwaz shows, separation can lead to stasis and negative egocentric behavior for those who do not have a sense of the need to work in the wider world or a sense of responsibility to the community and the family.

This rune is also the title of one of the most important Vanic gods, Freyr, the male fertility god. The *OERP* tells of this aspect and that Freyr often travels eastward into the sunrise (and twilight), which is the realm of giants and the force of nonconsciousness. This furthers the work of the Æsir through confrontation with the unconscious forces that threaten the worlds and is an exemplary model for those who would be heroes and leaders.

In this warrior-king aspect, Ingwaz is the rune of the ancestral/divine king. In the Germanic world, kings among men were thought to receive their power from the gods. They were responsible for good harvest (a connection with Jera, also under Freyr) and peace. The Anglo-Saxon kings traced their ancestry back to Woden, the Norse kings to Odin, and the Swedish to Ingvi-Freyr.

In a practical sense, the Ingwaz rune deals with the storing and transforming of energy. It is therefore useful to keep it in mind if you are putting ideas away for a rainy day or building up resources or ideas for a project to be sent forth in the future.

INGWAZ EXERCISES

Galdra

Ingwaz Ingwaz Ingwaz
Ing-Ing-Ing
Inga-Inga-Inga
Ingwaz Ingwaz Ingwaz

Magical uses

- Storing and transforming energy for personal use
- Meditation

Things to do

1. Isolate yourself for one weekend, perhaps on a retreat somewhere, to study the runes. When the weekend is over, record in your runic journal the benefits of your isolation.
2. Cultivate your personal energy. Develop your intellectual abilities.

Thoughts to meditate upon

1. What "seeds" have I planted in the world?
2. How does separation from the world help me to focus?
3. What can I transform into when I am separated?

Three ways to enact Ingwaz in your life

1. Use some physical form to illustrate runic energy. Examples could be runic yoga, martial arts, or body training through dance or gym work.
2. Tie up loose ends. Do not fritter away your energy on too many things or on needless worries or tasks. Think like a sovereign—delegate!

DAGAZ

Name Dagaz—Day

Alternative shapes

Number 23

Keywords Rune of the great Odinic consciousness, the synthesizing of opposite ideas, rune of deeper understanding and of enlightenment.

Rune poem stanza

D (Day) is the lord's messenger,   dear to men,
the ruler's famous light;   it is mirth and hope
to rich and poor,   and is useful for all.
OERP

MEANING

Dagaz, the day rune, enables you to perceive things from a wiser position. Expand your horizons. This rune is the coming together of extremes to form a dynamic synthesis that both complements and transcends the two initial states. This paradoxical operation is the mark of the Odinic state of mind. His followers know that Odin is the "Changeable One" and that they should expect the unexpected. The higher Odinic consciousness can be awakened in the mind through the combination of reason and rune work. Dagaz then becomes a shining light in the mind, revealing deeper understanding.

In the runic system, the synthesis of opposites often acts as a catalyst. The initial creation of the universe occurred through the coming together of Cosmic Fire and Ice. Much rune work uses this type of synthesis; the work is especially useful when it yokes objective knowledge with the subjective understanding of an initiate.

Dagaz is the rune of the seeker after mysteries. The work of the seeker further illuminates the mind and at the same time broadens the horizons so that there is even more mystery. This rune also makes the work of other seekers more understandable, so that the rune worker can benefit from this. Using this rune will also help the rune worker to overcome any (perhaps unconscious) limitations that other seekers have built into their own systems.

The rune journey never ends. With the runes, the seeker will unravel secrets that lead from one rune to another. The horizons of the known will expand and yet the call of the unknown will become stronger and more mysterious.

Hail Day!
Hail Day's sons!
Hail Night and her daughter!
SIGDRÍFUMÁL, 2

DAGAZ EXERCISES

Galdra
Dagaz Dagaz Dagaz/Da-Da-Da-Da/Daaaaaaaaa/Dagaz Dagaz Dagaz

Magical uses
• Synthesis of opposites
• Development of Odinic perspective

Things to do
1. Seek the mysteries. Bring back to the world what you find—share your wisdom.
2. Investigate institutions that worship Odin and those that seek to emulate rather than worship him.

Thoughts to meditate upon
1. What are the limits of my knowledge?
2. How can I extend what I know?
3. Am I truly awake? How would I know this?
4. How can I become more so?
5. When does the journey end?

Three ways to enact Dagaz in your life
1. Put your runic understanding to use. Solve problems that require objective knowledge with personal experience.
2. Involve yourself in something useful to all. One example would be to use your skills in something that benefits the community, such as the environmental movement.
3. Take something you think you know about, such as a political position or a social problem, and explore its opposite position. What can this teach you?

OTHALA

Name Othala—Ancestral property, homeland

Alternative shapes

Number 24

Keywords Rune of ancestral homeland, freedom, and well-being. The sanctuary where one can truly grow.

Rune poem stanza

> O (Estate) is very dear   to every man,
> if he can enjoy what is right   and according to custom
> in his dwelling,   most often in prosperity.
> OERP

MEANING

The Othala rune is the rune of the ancestral estate. It is the last rune in the row and represents the fulfillment of one journey and yet the starting point for further journeys.

Othala is a sacred place. This is the homeland and the hearth as well as the inner home of the self. The shape of Othala resembles a fortified enclosure with a well-defended gate. This makes it easy for friends and welcome guests to enter and for meeting outsiders on one's own terms. Unfriendly others will be met with an impenetrable barrier.

The concept of one's own space is important to the independent-minded person in early times. The estate symbolizes the sense of well-being and the freedom that comes from having a base from which to venture forth. In the homeland we are safe to be who we really are, away from the many masks that we often have to wear in the outside world. As self-expression is assured here, the home is also a good place for developing and refining skills in any art or craft.

Places of worship are also symbolized by this rune. Sacred groves acted as the temples in the old Germanic religions. The natural world provided many inspiring and holy places used by the Germanic peoples for worship. In later periods, temples to the Elder gods became widespread and include the famed Temple to Odin, Freyr, and Thor at Uppsala, Sweden. This was one of the last heathen temples of the Elder Ways, practicing until conversion in 1100 C.E.

Iceland also had temples, and there is a fascinating account of a follower of Thor, Thorulf, who dismantled his temple completely and migrated with it to Iceland, where he reerected it and sanctified it. The Othala rune also wards modern-day temples across the world to the old Germanic gods.

Othala is a rune that is closely associated with ideas of ancestral heritage, of pride in one's traditions, family, clan, and culture. In the old Northern traditions, the dead were often thought to be reborn into the ancestral line, which was often symbolized by the child taking the name of a dead grandparent or other relative.

Pride in ancestry does not exclude the value of the heritage of others, but also symbolizes meaningful exchanges with other clans, families, traditions, and cultures. Such exchanges were quite frequent in ancient times. People traveled across the known world, from North America to Russia, the Black Sea, and the Mediterranean.

Othala is also the rune of the wise management of resources, especially those things inherited or wealth that is not mobile (see Fehu, pages 54 57)—such as land, natural resources, and also the environment.

OTHALA EXERCISES

Galdra

Othala Othala Othala/Ooooooooooo/Ooooooooooo/Othala Othala Othala

Magical uses

• Celebrating and understanding ancestral heritage
• Finding roots
• Wealth and prosperity

Things to do

1. Set up a house-shrine at or near your hearth. This should contain a candle, some pictures of your ancestors, and a small bowl for offerings to the house spirits. Visit it daily.
2. Which movements seek to make our society a freer place, where religious and cultural differences can be celebrated?
3. Seek a dialogue with others who are not students of the runes about the belief system the runes involve. Seek to banish misconceptions politely.

Thoughts to meditate upon

1. Where is my homeland?
2. What does my home mean to me?
3. What do my ancestors teach me?

Three ways to enact Othala in your life

1. Seek great works in the world. Look at your answer to question 2 above. Seek to support movements that give us more freedom to practice our cultural and religious ways as we will.
2. Practice home crafts. Set about creating an ideal home with your own crafts.
3. Cultivate the house and hearth as the center of family life. See *True Hearth* in Further Reading, page 185, and seek other books of this type.

CHAPTER FIVE

RUNIC DIVINATION

Learn how to use the runes to answer questions in your life.

Your careful study of the runes in earlier chapters has prepared you for an introduction to the skill of divination using the runes. In this chapter you will learn the practices of rune casting and rune reading—how to draw rune staves from a pouch or lot box and find meaningful messages in the staves you have drawn.

The runes are the mysteries of the universe. Rune divination is about becoming attuned and sensitized to these mysteries, so that when you ask a question you can "read them aright" and understand their interconnections with all worlds.

Divination with the runes cannot show you what is predetermined to happen—predestination is not a part of the runic worldview. However, with this skill you can learn about your subjective, inner world—the mind and the heart.

FATE AND DIVINATION

Divination with the runes is underpinned by the concept of the Greater Norns, mythological women of destiny (see Chapter Three). These three "women of fate" are symbols of the past, the present, and the future: that which has happened, that which is coming into being, and that which should happen. Wyrd, or Fate, links these principles. In the runic view of time, the Norns weave together actual time, synchronicity, cause and effect, and the eternal, timeless world of myth.

Fate is not always positive. To be human is to accept the pleasures and pains of existence. The Norns bring both. An inscription in a Norwegian stave church illustrates this: "Norns brought great sorrow to me." We all have some sorrow in our lives; how we cope with this helps to determine whether we can fulfill the runic promise that leads us ever onward.

It was often believed that the Germanic peoples were resigned to their *wyrd*. However, it is more correct to assume that the ancient Germans, like traditional peoples everywhere, did practice divination and related arts and so were more in tune with their fate than is believed.

The questions you ask are important for rune divination. When you ask your question, you are inviting a response from the runes. In the next section, you will learn ways to seek meaningful answers. You will learn how to make your own rune staves and rune cards and use these for framing your questions.

CREATING RUNE STAVES

You will need some rune staves for divination work. Traditionally, these were made of wood. *Voluspá* 20 speaks of the Norns carving staves on wood. However, the staves may also be made out of bone, another organic substance, or even precious or semiprecious metals.

Why wood for rune staves? There are a number of traditional reasons:
1. Humans were created out of wood in the mythology.
2. Wood is organic—alive.
3. Runes were known to have been carved out of wood.

Runes can also be made out of wood-derived items such as cardboard. It is a good idea to create a set of rune cards first and practice with these while you collect the wood and plan to create a wooden set.

Although you do not need any woodworking experience, making wooden staves still requires careful work. Your efforts will mean that your runes are personalized and this will help to give you a deeper reading.

If, for some reason, you cannot create a set of rune cards, stores that sell runic books often stock good sets. Try to find a wooden, cardboard, or metal set—avoid plastic, crystal, or clay runes if possible. You can even get results from runes made out of shortbread cookies, but if you seek to be traditional, using the older forms is preferable.

RUNE CARDS

Rune cards are useful for practicing runes and for meditation and are easy to carry with you. To create a set of rune cards, you will need the following:
• sheets of stiff cardboard;
• a red ink pen/calligraphy marker, or red ocher paint (or you can make your own simply from powdered red ocher and linseed oil); and
• a ruler.

1. Choose a size for your cards, preferably three inches by four inches. Measure and cut out the cards neatly with a hobby knife.
2. Select a rune. Draw or paint it on the card. As you do so, visualize a red stream of rune might flowing from your inner being to the rune.
3. Sing the Galdra (see Chapter Four) of the rune as you color it and then speak the appropriate stanza from the rune poems for each rune. When you finish each one, recite: "Rune-might hold the holy runes."
4. You may wish to embellish the cards with a border, the full name of the rune in runic or English, and especially if you are not as yet used to the order of the runes, its number. You could place a holy sign on the back of the card.

Example of a Fehu rune card

WOODEN STAVES

You can make two types of wooden staves:

a) **Small disks**: Saw a branch into twenty-four sections of about a quarter-inch thickness. The best wood is from a fruit-bearing tree, but when you are starting out, any wood you can practice with is better than none. If you are not good with tools, try a softer wood at first.

b) **Rune lots**: Make from thin sheets of wood, available from a hardware or hobby store. These are quite compact, two to three inches long. If you carve these, carve lightly. They can also be painted.

You will need a carving knife or hobby knife to carve the staves. If you are cutting them from a tree or branch, you will need a small saw. If you are taking your branch from a tree, thank the Wight of the tree and tell it what rune(s) you are going to use the wood for. If you live in the city, suitable wood may be obtained from craft and hardware stores.

 ## CREATING THE STAVES

1. Before carving, hallow your work area and the runes-to-be with the Hammer Working on page 30.
2. Carve your runes against the grain of the wood. This will make them readable without coloring and will enable you to make the runes angular, a traditional property.
3. Choose which rune you wish to carve.
4. As you carve, visualize a red stream of rune might flowing from your inner being to the rune.
5. Carve away from your body to avoid being cut. If you are a beginner, it may help to first draw the runes with a light pencil stroke. Then cut with precise, controlled strokes. Smooth the rune with the edge of your blade or an awl.
6. If you make a mistake carving the rune (this may well happen), sand or whittle away the error.
7. Color the rune with paint or ocher to give it aesthetic charm and load it with rune might. Now repeat from Rune Cards, step 3, page 152.

RUNE CASTING

Casting runes means posing a question and then selecting staves randomly from a large number of runes. The symbols of those selected are interpreted to formulate the answer. Casting runes not only helps you to understand the question at hand, but also reenacts the Elder ways, quickening your ancestral wisdom.

The oldest account of Germanic divination is in Tacitus's *Germania*, written in 98 C.E. To cast runes, you will need:

- rune cards or rune tines—staves carved with runes,
- a white cloth about two feet by two feet, and
- a lot box (a box or other container) to draw the runes from; it should be big enough for shuffling the runes. (To shuffle, you could also spread all of the runes upside down on the white cloth and mix them thoroughly.)

When you cast the runes, ask your question in as few words as possible. Be specific and focused. Have your question prepared beforehand and make it unambiguous. For example, rather than asking "What should I do?" ask "Should I accept the job in Austin?"

THREE RUNE METHOD

The Three Rune Method is the most traditional and best-known rune divination method. It is the easiest to learn and the most useful.

1. Spread your white cloth so that one edge faces north. Place a cushion or stool on the south edge, where you can sit while reading the runes.
2. Perform a Hammer Working as on page 30.
3. Call the attention of the Norns. A good way to do so is to recite this stanza from the *Voluspá*:

    From there come the maidens
    with knowledge of many things
    three from that sea,
    which stands beneath the tree;
    one is called Urdhr,

the other Verdhandi,
they carved on sticks,
Skuld the third.
They laid down the law,
they choose the lives
of the children of men,
the fates of men
VOLUSPÁ 20

4. Shuffle your rune cards or rune tines. Think about your question. When you feel ready and are certain that the cards or tines are shuffled enough, speak your question out loud. Then say, "Runes rown right rede!"

5. Draw out three runes from the lot box. As you draw out the first, say "Urdhr," (that which has become). With the second, say "Verdhandi" (that which is becoming), and with the third, "Skuld" (that which shall be). Place the runes in order on the edge of the cloth so that you will know which one is related to which Norn.

6. Next it is traditional to call upon Odin to inspire you to read the runes to the best of your ability. A simple formula is, "Odin, may I read the runes aright!"

7. Sit on your stool or cushion.

8. Read the runes (see the next section) and come to an answer.

9. Record your results and your interpretation of them in your runic journal.

10. Finish by speaking the last verse of *Hávamál*:

Now are Hár's [Odin's] sayings said in Hár's Hall.
helpful to the sons of men,
but of no help to sons of Etins.
Hail the one who speaks them   hail the one who knows them,
Gain, the one who grasps them
hail those who hear them!

NINE RUNE METHOD (ADVANCED)

The Nine Rune Method is an extension of the Three Rune Method. There are several variants. The one we will look at here is based on the ninefold soul-lore model (see Chapter Three, page 41). Practice this method only after you are comfortable with the Three Rune Method, as it will take more practice and rune-reading skills to "read the runes aright." Use this method if you would like to gain insight into a question that relates to your inner life—the world of ideas, dreams, inspirations, and emotions.

The casting method is exactly the same as for the Three Rune Method, except that when you draw out each rune, you will need to speak the name of the part of the self that you are drawing.

One of the symbols that represents this Odian approach to consciousness is the **Valknut**, which is based on three interlocking triangles. Place each rune on one corner of the triangle.

The Nine Rune Method

1. **Hamingja**—personal power, luck, guardian spirit
2. **Lyke/Lich (body)**—interaction of mind and body, fitness, health
3. **Hyde**—"shape of body," which is changeable. Body image, shape-shifting
4. **Hugh**—intellect/analytical powers
5. **Myne**—reflection, memories, ancestral qualities
6. **Athem**—breath of life
7. **Wode**—inspiration
8. **Fetch**—following spirit; Jungian anima/animus and animal aspect of self
9. **Shade**—the shadow side of self

RUNE READING

In practical terms, what you are doing in rune reading is actively processing the runic connections between your inner world and the outer one. This is the basic theory of rune casting. By casting runes, we can understand our inner and outer worlds better. The accuracy of the results of the casting will depend on:

- how strongly you need to know the answer to the question,
- your understanding of the lore of the runes, and
- how complex your question is.

Here are some questions to ask yourself for each rune when you are doing a rune reading (this example is for a Three Rune Spread):

1. What does this rune mean?
2. What position is this rune in? How does it relate to the other positions?
3. How does this rune on its own relate to the question at hand?
4. How do the runes relate to the Nornic process (Three Rune Method)?
5. Taking into account each of the runes and each of the Nornic processes, how does this answer the question?
6. Which rune seems to answer my question best? Why?

The external forms of rune casting, such as choosing the runes, can distract from the reading process, so it is best to practice a few times beforehand so that the moves and actions become familiar. Once the actions become natural to you, you will then be focused totally on the more important internal process.

When you have cast the runes, read the explanations for the ones you have selected in Chapter Four or see the table at the end of this chapter. Read the rune poems associated with the runes. Think of how each selected rune relates to the Norn for which it has been drawn.

If your answer to the question you posed is negative, the tradition says that you should not ask any more runic questions that day.

Next, write or speak of what connections come to your mind after casting. After doing so, relate these thoughts in a meaningful way to the question that you posed. Your reading will require some pondering. The wisdom that you receive from rune reading may be simple and straightforward, but often it may be cryptic and masked. Whatever the result of your reading, write it in your runic journal, along with a note of the question posed. This record will be a valuable resource for your learning in the days, months, and years ahead.

A good reading will mean that you have read the runes correctly and have gained some worthwhile insight into your question. Your reading will "ring true." You should be able to test whether it is a good reading by what it enables you to do in Midgard—the world. If it was a good reading, you will be led to other actions ("one rune leads to another rune"). A poor reading will either lead you astray or have no effect. Only experience will teach you to recognize when you have "read aright."

WHEN TO CAST—TRADITIONAL

The best time to cast for yourself is at night. Night is when most of us have time to look inward and do not have to worry about the toils of the daytime. You can also do personal rune casting on significant anniversaries or other occasions, such as birthdays, weddings, and graduations.

If you are part of a rune-study group, you may wish to incorporate rune casting into the calendar of Ásatrú festivals. These dates refer to the Northern Hemisphere, as this was the dwelling place of the ancient Germanic peoples:

Winter Nights—October 13–15

Yuletide—December 20–31 (including Mother Night on December 20 and Yule on December 31)

Disting—February 14

Ostara—March 21

May Day—May 1

Midsummer—June 21

Things Tide—August 23

Harvest—September 23

READING FOR OTHERS

In the Elder tradition, the rune master would read for others. This would occur in times of great need, such as wartime, or in times of great celebration, such as a birth, significant birthday, or festival.

When your friends find out that you are studying runes, they may well ask you for a reading. Serving your community through your rune work is a worthy aspiration of the rune worker, but before you do so you will first need to feel confident in your ability to perform a good reading for yourself.

When reading for others, you will be attempting to apply the same process that you have used for readings about yourself. This can be very difficult, because it is hard to know the inner state of another. You can certainly use what you know about the person's background, motivations, and life. Use this sort of approach to gain a deeper understanding of the subject so that the reading can be more effective.

You should only read for a friend if both of you take the subject seriously. Rune reading is not a game. If you are in need of a Northern traditional game, try Tafl. It is an enjoyable game, the Viking equivalent of chess.

KNOWING YOUR WYRD

Why would we use runes to answer questions? Rune work seeks a balanced, holistic approach to the mysteries of the self and the universe. This awakened, illuminated perspective (see Dagaz, pages 142–145) implies knowing not only who and what you are, but where you are going and who you want to be. To know your Wyrd means to have the chance to see where you are going and to have a sense of purpose and vitality—a goal that you can seek. Additionally, if your Wyrd shows much rough weather, you may be able to act to minimize or avoid catastrophe. Before you avoid a difficult situation, however, remember that we all need challenges. Too much comfort leads to stasis.

From this perspective, remember that we do not need to use runes to explore the known. If you know what course of action to take, take it. Runes are for illumining the unknown, for helping you decide a path when there seems to be too few or too many choices.

RUNE-READING TABLE

Here is a summary of the lore found in Chapter Four.

ᚠ	Energy, wealth, new beginnings	ᛊ	Traveling the World Tree, life and death
ᚢ	Strength, vitality, organic	ᛈ	Communication with the divine realm, danger
ᚦ	Will, reactive force, Thor	ᛉ	Chance, synchronicity, Norns, transformation
ᚨ	Mind, self, Odin, communication	ᛋ	Goal, good counsel, individual success
ᚱ	Riding, pathway, reason	ᛏ	Victory, truth, balance
ᚲ	Creativity, shaping, art	ᛒ	Liberation, energy release, birth and rebirth
ᚷ	Gift, sacrifice, hospitality	ᛗ	Teamwork, friendship, trust
ᚹ	Joy, harmony, well-being	ᛗ	Awareness, awakening, potential
ᚻ	Crisis, stress, storm	ᛚ	Life force, healing, quickening
ᚾ	Need, test, ordeal	ᛜ	Hiding, separation, gestation
ᛁ	Contraction, stillness, silence	ᛞ	Paradox, Odinic consciousness, synthesis
ᛃ	Good harvest, fruit, feast, cycles	ᛟ	Ancestral home, well-being, sanctuary

WORKBOOK EXERCISES

1. Do a reading of a Three Rune Method for yourself. Start by following steps 1–7 from the Three Rune Method (see pages 154–155). Before proceeding to step 8, take a moment to meditate on the runes you have chosen and their positionings. In your runic journal, write down your thoughts on what answer you think the runes are giving you.

2. a) Now read the meaning of the rune in the "Urdhr" position (refer to page 192 for quick reference). You should read this rune in regard to the past ("that which has become"). How does this rune relate to the question at hand?

   b) Read the rune in the "Verdhandi" position in relation to the present ("that which is becoming"). How does this rune relate to the question at hand?

   c) Read the meaning of the rune in the "Skuld" position in regard to the future ("that which shall be"). How does this rune relate to the question at hand?

3. Now read the positions together by asking yourself the following questions:
   a) How does each rune relate to the other positions?
   b) How does this spread answer the question? Write your answer in your runic journal. Compare this answer with what you wrote down for question 1. Are there similarities? What does this tell you?

4. Continue to practice doing readings for yourself using the Three Rune Method. When you feel comfortable with your ability, try doing a reading for yourself using the advanced Nine Rune Method (see page 156). Remember to read each rune in relation to the individual position it occupies in the spread, how it relates to the other positions, and how it relates to the question at hand.

5. When you feel confident of your ability to perform a good reading for yourself, try doing a reading for a friend or family member. Follow the same steps as you would when doing a reading for yourself. Write down your experiences of this in your runic journal, for example: What was successful about the reading? What was unsuccessful? What would you do differently in your next reading? What would you do the same? Follow this process for each reading you do.

6. Update your runic journal (see page 12).

CHAPTER SIX

RUNE MAGIC

T his chapter outlines the practice of that most mysterious art of Odin—of using runes for magical ends. It also gives an overview of the magical paths that make up the current revival of the Northern ways—the way of Galdra, or rune magic.

A SYMBOLIC INTERACTION

Magic is a means of symbolic interaction of the self with itself or with the objective world to cause or prevent changes. Change occurs through the use of symbolic forms, by means of willed acts of communication with paranormal forces. In magic it is the will of the individual magician that is of prime consideration, whereas in religion the community attempts to modify its behavior to the external standards of a god or gods. Rune magic is a way to achieve willed goals and enact the runes in our lives in a truly transformative way. Through the use of such magical arts as Galdra, rune sending, and rune talismans, the rune magician can deepen his or her knowledge of the runes.

As you have learned thus far, the runes are a communicative tool that can help illuminate your core self and help you to understand your Wyrd and the whole mythological universe of the Germanic peoples. Rune magic can also help you learn more about your own psychology—your "self-lore." When the runes speak to you, you are participating in the mysterious world of living tradition. This can be a source of great personal power and even a life-changing experience.

Rune magic centers on the self of the individual magician and combines this with a holistic approach. It requires:

- a strong focus on self-awareness,
- honesty about your capabilities,
- the ability to become inspired, and
- a strong commitment to seeking the mysteries, as with all rune work.

A PRACTICAL MAGIC

The types of magic described in the runic lore are very practical and worldly. Magic for the Germanic peoples was neither an abstract nor an academic interest. It was result based and focused on real-world issues such as:

- overcoming sickness,
- finding opportunities to be able to use one's abilities to the fullest,
- dealing with injustices, and
- helping with the affairs of the heart.

These are some of the types of magic practiced by the rough-and-ready rune magician, Egil Skallagrímsson, in *Egil's Saga*.

Odin is the patron of rune magic. His ways and quests are models for modern rune magicians. His is the example to be followed for important tasks such as rune initiation, rune casting, and the shaping of self-consciousness. Knowledge of Odin's ways can be found in the *Edda*, especially the mythological texts, such as *Hávamál*.

A SOUND-BASED MAGIC

Galdra, the word for magical chanting of the runes, indicates the importance of sound in this type of magic. As mentioned earlier, the word means "to crow like a raven." Verbal aspects of rune magic are as important as the visual signs of the runes. Magical chantings release knowledge of the runes. This is why it is important to learn the rune poems, rune names, and Galdra chants for the runes.

PREPARING THE RUNES

Carving the runes is an essential part of rune magic. From Chapter Five, you should have a good idea of how to carve, color, and load the runes for divination. As mentioned in that chapter, divination is a type of magic enacted to gain knowledge. Your experience with divination will give you a good grounding for the more active works of rune magic.

 ## TAKING UP THE RUNES

Before you can use the runes to cause change, you will need to take them up for yourself. To do this, systematically work through all of the twenty-four Futhark runes as described in Chapter Four. Do the following for each rune, taking three nights to do so:

1. Perform the Hammer Working on page 30.
2. Read the rune poem(s) for the rune.
3. Meditate on each rune for ten to thirty minutes per night.
4. At the end of the meditation, visualize the rune in glowing red light in your core being.

 ## RUNE SENDING

When you think that you know the runes deeply enough, you may start to "send" in order for them to cause change in your subjective or objective world. To do so:

1. Find the rune that most closely matches your goal and again visualize it in glowing red light in your core being.
2. Holding up a stave, your rune-carving knife, or just your hand, visualize the rune streaming along the object and being made manifest in the world.
3. At the same time, intone the Galdra associated with the rune (see Chapter Four).
4. Then imagine that the rune has caused the change you need.
5. With practice, and if you really need what you are trying to achieve, you will get results.
6. In your runic journal, write the aim of your sending. Later, write the results.

TALISMANS AND FORMULAS

Another important aspect of rune magic is the construction of rune talismans. These are often empowered with formulas, as mentioned in Chapters One, Two, and Four. They could be used with single runes or with bind runes to combine the powers of several of the runes. Magical rune tines should be hidden around your work area as talismans or worn under clothing as appropriate. If you have carved your tine in wood, you can make a small hole carefully with a knife and awl or using a drill.

Here are some formulas that are often used in rune inscriptions. They can be adapted for Galdra, for other forms of rune magic, or for talismans.

- **Alu**: This word means "ale" and signifies magical potency, inspiration, and might. An example of its use is on the Körlin ring inscription (see page 48).
- **Gibo Auja**: This means "I give protection." This formula is often represented by a bind rune (see page 46).
- **Laukaz**: This means "leek." This formula invokes the power of the Laguz rune, especially in the life-promoting aspect of the leek plant. This quick-growing plant symbolizes fertility, growth, and increase.
- **Ek Erilaz**: This is the rune-master formula: "I, the rune master." This formula may aid those who aspire to master the runes. As the formula is an advanced one, you may want to try it after mastering the rest of this book. One such formula is from the Kragehul spear shaft from Denmark (see page 15). Note that this inscription contains three bind runes of **Gibo Auja**. When carving this formula, replace the name of the rune master **Ansugisalaz** with your own name. If you have joined a rune workers' group, you may have taken a traditional Germanic name. Use this name for the formula.
- **Holy signs**: You may also want to incorporate some of the Northern holy signs into your talisman. You could take a design from the *Galdrabók* tradition. If you have some artistic skill (and most people do in a latent form), you may want to try to work the piece along the lines of one of the artistic styles known to the heathen world.

The Gibo Auja
bind rune

HELM OF AWE TALISMANS

The Helms of Awe, or *Aegishjálmur*, from the Icelandic *Galdrabók* traditions, were talismanic designs that often incorporated runic signs or ideas to influence events or the user. They are mentioned in the *Volsunga* saga, in which the Helm of Awe was used by the dragon Fáfnir to cause uncontrollable fear in his foes.

The Helms of Awe in the Icelandic material are often used for increasing power generally, but also can be used for specific aims. For example, the Helm of Awe *Ginnfaxi* was used for strength, especially in wrestling contests.

Some other Helms of Awe are:

1. The basic Helm of Awe—for increase of power in all realms.
2. *Ginnur*—called "Holy." This stave is designed to protect the self and increase one's powers in the outside world.
3. *Angurgapi*. Sometimes carved into barrels, this could chase away vermin and other misfortunes. Extremely protective, slightly ominous, and very potent, it contains twenty-four tines (the number of runes in the Elder Futhark).

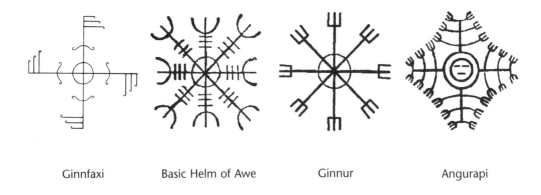

Ginnfaxi   Basic Helm of Awe   Ginnur   Angurapi

A RUNE MAGIC REVIVAL

THE ARMANEN RUNES

The first revival of rune magic occurred in the late nineteenth century through the efforts of Völkish magician Guido von List. A spiritual experience when recovering from a cataract operation led him to develop a new rune row called the *Armanen* Runes. The magical aspects of these were explored through the Armanen Order, which he founded in 1911. This innovative order incorporated into the rune system material from other traditions, such as the Stadha, or rune yoga.

Until the 1930s Germanic mythology was very popular. Runes and ancient gods were everywhere, from Wagner's operas to advertising, architecture, popular novels, drama, and public sculpture. Rune magic became a focal point. Other rune magicians inspired by von List include Siegfried Adolf Kummer, Friedrich Bernhard Marby, and Karl Maria Wiligut. Armanen Runes became a part of the general occult milieu and were also taught in magical orders such as the Fraternitas Saturni. Odinist religious groups sprang up in many countries.

The Armanen Runes

THE SECOND RUNIC REVIVAL

Later, in the early 1970s, the runic movement was again revived, with movements such as the *Ásatrúarmenn* founded by Sveinbjörn Beinteinsson in Iceland, which received government recognition as a religion in 1973. In the UK, the Odinic Rite was founded at this time by John Yeowell, and in the United States, the Ásatrú Free Assembly (AFA) was founded by Stephen McNallen. These three groups developed what was to become modern Ásatrú. Though far from agreeing on all details of the reconstruction, they paved the way for the multitude of groups following the Northern tradition that exist in the first decade of the twenty-first century.

From the greater Ásatrú field, the organization called the Rune Gild emerged in 1980, mainly from members of the AFA and Odinic Rite who were interested in runes as a magical and initiatory path. Ongoing exploration into the complex of the self is a hallmark of the Rune Gild. The Rune Gild is not Odinist—it does not worship Odin, but is "Odian," which means that Gilders seek to emulate Odin—to seek what he seeks and to take up the runes as he did (see page 37).

MAGIC IN THE VANIR REALM: VANATRU AND SEIDHR

Rune magic represents only one of the magical traditions of the North. It is focused on the god Odin, who was not the favorite god of the North, often accused of being mysterious and grim. Another magical tradition of the North is one that falls under the rule of the Vanir gods—the gods of fertility, reproduction, and the natural world and its cycles. The most famous of these Vanic gods are Freyja and Freyr (the Lady and the Lord). There are currently two main traditions of Vanir-focused magic, **Vanatru,** or *wiccecræft* (witchcraft), and *Seidhr* (see Further Reading, page 185). Seidhr is connected with Freyja, the goddess linked with eroticism, fertility, and love. It is interesting to note that Freyja teaches these arts to Odin. Once you are advanced in your rune work, you may wish to study Seidhr for the light it can throw on runic lore.

WORKBOOK EXERCISES

1. Make a **rune talisman**. Start by writing in your runic journal your aim in making the talisman. Use the runes for a specific result or in order to understand them better. Now plan the inscription. You could:

   • Use a rune formula if one matches your goal. Choose the formula from the list on page 165 or from your reading.

   • Use a holy sign.

   • Copy a runic inscription from this book, perhaps in a design incorporating a holy sign.

   • Keep in mind the intended aesthetic effect of the talisman. The more concise the talisman, the better. Also, it will be easier to carve.

   Create the talisman using the process of creating a wooden rune stave from Chapter Five. Work out beforehand how much room you will need for the inscription. It may help you to make a light tracing of the inscription first with a pencil. Once you have made and used the talisman, record any results you have noticed.

2. Make a **Helm of Awe talisman**, following these steps:

   • Choose some wood, as on page 153, or select a specially prepared or potent sheet of paper (something from an art store, substantial and aesthetically pleasing to you, will have this effect).

   • Do the Hammer Working (see page 30).

   • Use the general procedures for rune carving given on page 153. If using paper, use red or black ink.

   • Visualize the Helm of Awe when carving or drawing it.

   • To complete the task, put the talisman in the place to which it relates. You could hide it there. If the talisman is for a personal matter, wear it or carry it with you. If it relates to your house, hide it above the door.

3. Update your runic journal (see page 12).

Rune magic is a difficult skill to learn. However, with perseverance, a grounding in the tradition, and a pragmatic approach, results will come to those who follow the way of Odin.

CHAPTER SEVEN

LORE AND LITERATURE

Learn about the runes in prose, poetry, and inscriptions.

Our earliest knowledge of the runes is from inscriptions and poems. Now that you have learned the basics of the runic system, it is time to explore its use in the written language. This chapter provides extracts from the runic literature of the earliest times and from inscriptions using runes. As you read these texts, you will become aware of the complexity of the runes. They function as symbols, relating to timeless themes relevant to all humans. Workbook exercises are provided to help you relate the ancient wisdoms to your own present, develop your self-awareness, and learn how to use your own energies creatively.

RUNIC INSCRIPTIONS

Chapter One gives a brief overview of some of the inscriptions in runes. The inscriptions are evidence of the magical lore of the runes:

- They transport us to the age of the ancient Germanic peoples and allow us to share their worldview.
- They help us to understand how mythology was incorporated into the lives of these ancient peoples. For example, Thor's hammer is used to hallow the inscription on the Sønder Kirkby Stone.
- They provide some potent formulas for the rune worker to use.

The rune inscriptions are the earliest textual accounts we have of the lore of the Northern tradition. The inscriptions often supplement later mythological material or help to give an understanding of how the runes were used. An example of this is the use of the

Thor's hammer to hallow the inscription on the Sønder Kirkby Stone. This use of the Thor's hammer has some evidence in the *Edda*.

Inscriptions were carved on standing stones, weapons, jewelry, and also on wooden objects (many of which would have perished, as wood does not last well). A special type of inscription is found on the coin-sized gold disks known as bracteates. These are probably related to the religion of Odin. Many of the bracteates have magical formulas.

One inscription that is relevant to this study is on the Darum bracteate 5, which has the inscription **Alu Niujill**. This can be interpreted as "Protective Magic, Newcomer." It contains the potent formula **Alu**, which was a form of protective magical power (see pages 48–49). Possibly it is designed to be worn by a child or an apprentice rune magician.

 WORKBOOK EXERCISE

Create an inscription. Using the instructions in Chapter Five on rune carving, carve "Alu Niujill" (ᚠᛚᚢ ᚾᛁᚢᛇᛁᛚᛚ). Intone the runes and visualize them in red as you carve them. You may also practice inscribing any of the other formulas mentioned in this book, such as the "Gibo Auji" formula (see page 165).

A CONTINUING STUDY

New runic inscriptions are frequently found on archaeological digs. These help to increase our knowledge of the runes. If you are interested, you could subscribe to an archaeological journal and visit museums where rune artifacts are kept. Any new inscriptions found add to the current knowledge base of the lore. As a rune worker, you will always be on the path of learning.

THE RUNE POEMS

Three rune poems are of particular interest to the rune worker. These are the *Old English Rune Poem* (OERP), *Old Norwegian Rune Poem* (ONRP), and *Old Icelandic Rune Poem* (OIRP), so named because of the languages in which they are written. The rune poems are extremely important to our understanding of the runes. They contain many layers of meaning and provide exemplary forms for rune Galdra and poetry.

These poems function for the modern rune worker similarly to koans in the Zen Buddhist tradition, where poetic forms are meditated upon to unravel their hidden meaning. This is especially true of the *ONRP*, as the second stanza for each rune, though unrelated in subject matter, is considered to be a different aspect of the first. The *OIRP* also has a Latin summary at the bottom, which helps us understand the overall meaning.

The text of the rune poems is useful to meditate on for each particular rune. The poems also bear much beauty and wisdom when read in sequence.

 ## WORKBOOK EXERCISES

Meditate on the following translations of the rune poems, then ask yourself the following questions:

1. What does this poem mean to me?
2. How can it further my goals?
3. How can it show my blind spots?
4. What do I understand best about this poem?
5. What should I try to understand better about this poem?
6. How can it tell me more about the runes?

As always, keep detailed notes of all of these questions and answers in your runic journal.

Return to the rune poems whenever you want to gain deep insight into the runes.

You will notice in the following translations that the *OERP* contains the extra runes of the Anglo-Saxon/Frisian Runes. These are important in the context of the Anglo-Saxon/Frisian Rune Poem and for understanding the heathen English traditions, but the rune learner should concentrate on the Elder Futhark first. The *ONRP* and *OIRP* only contain the runes for the Younger Futhark. That aside, both of these poems are invaluable for understanding the Elder Futhark and form one of the cornerstones of the tradition.

OLD ENGLISH RUNE POEM

F (Wealth) is a comfort to   *every man*
although every man ought   *to deal it out freely*
if he wants, before the lord,   *his lot of judgment.*

U (Urus) is fearless   *and greatly horned*
a very fierce beast   *it fights with its horns,*
a famous roamer of the moor   *it is a courageous animal.*

TH (Thorn) is very sharp;   *for every thegn*
who grasps it, it is harmful   *and exceedingly cruel*
to every man   *who lies upon it.*

A (God) is the chieftain   *of all speech,*
the mainstay of wisdom   *and comfort to the wise,*
for every noble warrior   *hope and happiness.*

R (Riding) is in the hall, *to every warrior*
easy, but very hard   *for one who sits up*
on a powerful horse   *over the miles of road.*

K (Torch) is to every living person *known by its fire*
it is clear and bright   *it usually burns*
when the noble-men   *rest inside the hall.*

G (Gift) is for every man   *a pride and praise,*
help and worthiness;   *(and) of every homeless adventurer,*
it is the estate and substance   *for those who have nothing else.*

W (Joy) is had   by the one who knows few troubles
pains and sorrows,   and to him who himself has
power and blessedness,   and also the plenty of towns.

H (Hail) is the whitest of grains,   it comes from high in heaven.
A shower of wind hurls it,   then it turns to water.

N (Need) is constricting on the chest,
although to the children of men it often becomes
a help and salvation nevertheless
if they head it in time.

I (Ice) is very cold   and exceedingly slippery;
it glistens, clear as glass, very much like gems,
a floor made of frost   is fair to see.

J (Harvest) is the hope of men,   when god lets,
holy king of heaven,   the Earth give
her bright fruits   to the nobles and the needy.

EI (Yew) is, on the outside,   a rough tree
and hard, firm in the earth,   keeper of the fire,
supported by roots,   (it is a) joy on the estate.

P (Lot Box) is always   play and laughter
among bold men,   where the warriors sit
in the beer hall,   happy together.

Z (Elk's) sedge has its home   most often in the fen,
it waxes in the water   and grimly wounds,
and burns with blood   any bairn
who in any way   tries to grasp it.

S (Sun) is by sea-men   always hoped for
when they fare far away over the fishes' bath [sea],
until the brine-stallion [ship] they bring to land.

T (Tyr) is a token,   it keeps troth well
with noble-men   always on its course
over the mists of night, it never fails.

B (Birch) is without fruit   but just the same it bears
limbs without seed;   it has beautiful branches
high on its crown   it is finely covered
loaded with leaves,   touching the sky.

E (Horse) is, in front of the warriors,   the joy of noble-men,
a charger proud on its hooves;   when concerning it, heroes—
wealthy men—on war horses   exchange speech,
and it is always a comfort   to the restless.

M (Man) is in his mirth dear to his kinsman;
although each shall   depart from the other;
for the lord wants to commit,   by his decree,
that frail flesh   to the earth.

L (Water) is to people   seemingly unending,
if they should venture out   on an unsteady ship,
and the sea waves   frighten them very much,
and the brine-stallion   does not heed its bridle.

ING (Ing) was first   among   the East-Danes
seen by men,   until he again eastward
went over the wave;   the wain followed on;
this is what the warriors called the hero.

D (Day) is the lord's messenger,   dear to men,
the ruler's famous light;   it is mirth and hope
to rich and poor,   and is useful to all.

O (Estate) is very dear to every man,
if he can enjoy what is right   and according to custom
in his dwelling,   most often in prosperity.

(Oak) is on the Earth   for the children of men
the nourishment of meat;   it often fares
over the gannet's bath [sea]. The sea finds out
whether the oak keeps   noble troth.

(Ash) is very tall,   (and) very dear to men
standing on its base, it holds its stead rightly
though it is fought against   by many folks.

(Bow) is for nobleman   and warrior alike
a joy and dignification,   it is excellent on a horse,
steadfast on an expedition—(it is) a piece of war-gear.

(Serpent) is a river-fish   although it always takes
food on land,   it has a fair abode
surrounded with water,   where it lives in happiness.

(Grave) is hateful   to every warrior
when steadily   the flesh begins,
the corpse, to become cold,   to choose the earth
palely as a bed-mate; fruits fall
joys pass away,   bonds of faith break.

OLD NORWEGIAN RUNE POEM

F (Gold) causes strife amongst kinsmen;
the wolf grows up in the woods.

U (Slag) is from bad iron;
oft runs the reindeer on the hard snow.

TH (Thurs) causes the sickness of women;
few are cheerful from misfortune.

A (Estuary) is the way of most journeys;
but the sheath is (that way) for swords.

R (Riding), it is said, is the worst for horses;
Reginn forged the best sword.

K (Sore) is the curse of children;
grief makes a man pale.

H (Hail) is the coldest of grains;
Hropt shaped the world in ancient times.

N (Need) makes for a difficult situation;
the naked freeze in the frost.

I (Ice), we call the broad bridge;
the blind need to be led.

J (Harvest) is the profit of all men;
I say that Frodhi was generous.

S (Sun) is the light of the lands;
I bow to the doom of holiness.

T (Tyr) is the one-handed among the Æsir;
the smith has to blow often.

B (Birch-twig) is the limb greenest with leaves;
Loki brought the luck of deceit.

M (Man) is the increase of dust;
mighty is the talon-span of the hawk.

L (Water) is that which falls from the mountain
as a force; but gold (objects) are costly things.

Y (Yew) is the greenest wood in the winter;
there is usually, when it burns, singeing.

OLD ICELANDIC RUNE POEM

F (Gold) is strife among kinsmen   and fire of the flood tide
    and the path of the serpent.

    Gold.   "Leader of the war-band"

U (Drizzle) is the weeping of clouds and the lessener of the rim of ice
and the herdsman's hate.

    Shadow, or Shower.   "Leader"

TH (Thurs) is the torment of women   and the dweller in the rocks
    and the husband of the Etin-wife Vardh-runa.

    Saturn.   "Ruler of the Legal Assembly"

A (Ase) is the olden-father   and Asgard's chieftain
and the leader of Valhalla.

    Jupiter.   "Point-Leader"

R (Riding) is a blessed sitting   and a swift journey
and the toil of the horse.

    Journey.   "Worthy-man"

K (Sore) is the bale of children   and a scourge
    and the house of rotten flesh.

    Whip.   "King"

H (Hail) is a cold grain and a shower of sleet
and the bane of snakes.

    Hail.   "Battle-leader"

N (Need) is the grief of the bondmaid   and a hard condition
    and toilsome work.

Work.   "Descendant of the mist"
I (Ice) is the rind of the river   and the roof of the waves
and a danger for fey men.

        Ice.   "One who wears the boar helmet"

J (Harvest) is the profit of all men and a good summer
and a ripened field.

        Year.   "All-ruler"

S (Sun) is the shield of the clouds and a shining glory
and the life-long sorrow of ice.

        Wheel.   "Descendant of the victorious one"

T (Tyr) is the one-handed god   and the leavings of the wolf
and the ruler of the temple.

        Mars.   "Director"

B (Birch-twig) is a leafy limb   and a little tree
and a youthful wood.

        Silver fir.   "Protector"

M (Man) is the joy of man   and the increase of dust
and the adornment of ships.

        Human.   "Generous one"

L (Water) is a churning lake   and a wide kettle
and the land of fish.

        Lake.   "Praise-worthy one"

Y (Yew) is a strung bow and brittle iron
and a giant of the arrow.

        Bow.   "Descendant of Yngvi"

CHAPTER EIGHT

THE RUNES IN YOUR LIFE

Guidelines for an ethical life.

The ancient Germanic religion that pervades the runes—Ásatrú, or the Troth—has as its basis ethical principles that will enhance the life of a rune worker of any era. There are many similarities between Ásatrú rituals and rune working exercises, including magical exercises.

Ásatrú gives the rune worker a cultural, religious, and ethical dimension in which to develop. The ethics of Ásatrú are based on the *Eddas*. The Nine Noble Virtues are a condensation of the wisdom of the *Eddas*, and were first promoted by the Odinic Rite in the United Kingdom in the 1970s.

THE NINE NOBLE VIRTUES
1. **Courage** (heartiness)
2. **Truth**
3. **Honor** (worthiness)
4. **Fidelity** (troth)
5. **Discipline** (hardiness)
6. **Hospitality** (friendliness)
7. **Industriousness** (work)
8. **Self-reliance** (freedom)
9. **Perseverance** (steadfastness)

These virtues can give you ethical guidelines to keep in mind for all that you do. How they are applied depends entirely on your conscience and circumstances.

THE SIXFOLD GOAL

The Sixfold Goal was developed by the Ring of Troth movement as a condensation of ethical principles from the Northern tradition. The Sixfold Goal sets ethical goals for which to strive. The goal is:

1. Right
2. Wisdom
3. Might
4. Harvest
5. Frith (peace)
6. Love

Working toward these goals will give the runes a greater depth for the rune worker. These goals are all interrelated and all should be pursued.

KEEPING YOUR TROTH

As you have learned from beginning work with the runes, being true is central to well-being. Be steadfast in your words and deeds. If you make promises to people, keep them. If you swear oaths, keep them. It is better not to give your word on something than to give it falsely, as this will stain your personal honor.

 WORKBOOK EXERCISES

Think of the promises, agreements, or oaths you have made over the past couple of years.

1. Think about those oaths and promises you have kept. List them, and for each, list the feelings connected with the keeping of that oath: pride, relief, gladness, and so on. Which were difficult to keep? Why? Do you regret keeping to these oaths?

2. Have you broken any oaths? If so, how can you make amends? Write your thoughts in your runic journal.

THE RUNE-HOARD MEDITATION

This exercise is the last in this workbook. It gives you an opportunity to review your work and also provides you with advice about further paths to follow with your rune study.

You will need your runic journal, as well as your rune cards or staves.

Before you begin the meditation, reread the notes you have made in your runic journal while working through this workbook. Think about these questions:

1. Have your goals changed over time?
2. Have you completed any of your goals?
3. Have the runes been what you expected?

Then do the following:

1. Take a few minutes to think and write about a self-transformative goal you think you can achieve with the runes.
2. Do the Hammer Working (page 30).
3. Choose the rune for which you feel most affinity. Perform its Galdra (see Chapter Four).
4. Visualize the rune in glowing red. Do this for several minutes. Whisper your goal to yourself.
5. To complete this meditation, perform a rune casting for yourself or create a talisman to help with your goal, using the rune you chose.
6. Close the meditation.
7. Make notes in your runic journal. Keep using the journal as you continue your fascinating and self-revealing work with the runes.

AFTERWORD

Starting work on the runes means starting on a path that will never end. It is a path of constant learning, of the constant gaining of new insights into your self, the world you live in, and the world of your past. May this book have set you on the path and be your guide.

Keep working with the runes as often as you can. Rune wisdom is not something that will happen overnight. It is something to strive for. It cannot be learned from books; it comes only from seeking the mysteries of the runes and integrating them into your life.

Wisdom is watched over by Odin. This is the hidden lore and powers welling up from the darkest depths of our souls and hovering high over our heads, shining beyond the clouds and leading us on into the unknown. This is the mysterious force that has the ability to hold all things together, ruled by those who can see and understand the whole. Above all, wisdom must be preserved, for in it are the wells of memory; if and only if it survives, all other parts of the whole may be regenerated. From this is derived our sense of adventure, our curiosity about the unknown, our seeking and questing character.
—A BOOK OF TROTH

Reyn Til Runa!
(Seek the Mysteries!)

RESOURCES

For basic introductions to the runes, see your local university or community college for a grounding in objective lore, as well as the languages of the heathen past. Also, see institutions such as the Mimung Society, a cross-campus Indo-European focus group that encourages students to delve into our ancestral heritage. Woodharrow Institute is a school that teaches languages and Germanic cultural courses.

Current large-scale organizations include the Ásatrúarmenn, Ásatrú Folk Assembly, Rune Gild, and the Ring of Troth. If you are interested in joining any group, seek to resolve any questions or problems you may have with their approach. Many groups have informal meetings that you should be able to attend.

ORGANIZATIONS & SERVICES

Rune Gild
  www.runegild.org

Rûna-Raven Press
  www.runegild.org/runaraven1.html

Ásatrúarmenn—Iceland
  www.asatru.is

Odinic Rite
  www.odinic-rite.org

Ásatrú Folk Assembly
  www.runestone.org

The Troth (formerly Ring of Troth)
  www.thetroth.org

Hrafnar (Diana Paxson)
  www.hrafnar.org

Woodharrow Institute of Germanic & Runic Studies
  P.O. Box 557
  Smithville, TX 78957

Runa: Exploring Northern European Myth, Mystery &
  Magic (journal)
  BM Sorcery
  London WC1N 3XX
  UK

Tyr: Myth—Culture—Tradition (journal)
  ULTRA
  P.O. Box 11736
  Atlanta, GA 30355

Renewal (journal)
  P.O. Box 4333
  University of Melbourne
  Vic 3052
  Australia

Vor Tru (journal)
  P.O. Box 961
  Payson, AZ 85547

ACADEMIC ACKNOWLEDGMENTS

- The Rune Poems (OERP, ONRP, OIRP), Hávamál—Rúnatals appear courtesy Edred Thorsson, from *Nine Doors of Midgard*, Rûna-Raven Press, 2001 (2nd ed.).
- "Wisdom" from Edred Thorsson, *A Book of Troth*, Rûna-Raven Press, 2003 (2nd ed.).
- Prose Edda, Voluspá, Gylfaginnung, Havamál 145, Sigrífumal—original translations by Daniel Bray.
- Yggdrasil and Soul-lore diagrams by Edred Thorsson, from *Nine Doors of Midgard*, Rûna-Raven Press, 2001 (2nd ed.).

FURTHER READING

Antonsen, Elmer. *A Concise Grammar of the Older Runic Inscriptions*. Niemeyer Verlag, Germany, 1975.

Chisholm, James. *Grove and Gallows*. Rûna-Raven Press, TX, 2002.

——*True Hearth*. Rûna-Raven Press, TX, 1994 (2nd ed.).

Davidson, Hilda Ellis. *The Lost Beliefs of Northern Europe*. Routledge, UK, 1993.

Faulkes, Anthony. *Edda*. Everyman, London, 1987.

Fell, Christine (trans). *Egil's Saga*. Everyman's Library, UK, 1975.

Flowers, Stephen E. *Galdrabók: An Icelandic Grimoire*. Weiser, MN, 1989.

——*The Rune Poems*. Rûna-Raven Press, TX, 2002.

——*Runes and Magic*. Peter Lang, UK, 1986.

Hollander, Lee. *Poetic Edda*. University of Texas Press, TX, 1962.

——*The Skalds*. University of Michigan Press, MI, 1968.

Lindow, John. *Norse Mythology: A Guide to the Gods, Heroes, Rituals and Beliefs*. Oxford University Press, UK, 2001.

Molkte, Eric. *Runes and Their Origin: Denmark and Elsewhere*. National Museum of Denmark, Copenhagen, 1985.

Odenstedt, Bendt. *On the Origin and Early History of the Runic Script*. Almqvist & Wiksell, Sweden, 1990.

Page, R. I. *Norse Myths*. British Museum Publications, UK, 1990.

Simek, Rudolf. *Dictionary of Norse Mythology*. D.S. Brewer, UK, 1993.

Thorsson, Edred. *A Book of Troth*. Rûna-Raven Press, 2003 (2nd ed.).

——*At the Well of Wyrd*. Weiser, TX, 1988.

——*Futhark: A Handbook of Rune Magic*. Weiser, TX, 1984.

——*Nine Doors of Midgard*. Rûna-Raven Press, TX, 2001 (2nd ed.).

——*Northern Magic*. Llewellyn, MN, 1998 (2nd ed.).

——*Runelore*. Weiser, ME, 1987.

——*Rune-Song*. Rûna-Raven Press, TX, 1993.

——*Witchdom of the True*. Rûna-Raven Press, TX, 1999.

Zoller, Robert. *Skaldic Number Lore*. Rûna-Raven Press, TX, 1999.

GLOSSARY

Æsir: Gods of **Asgard**, specializing in sovereignty, physical force, and prowess.

Aett: The line of eight runes when the **Futhark** rune row is divided into three.

Anglo-Saxon/Frisian Runes: The extended set of runes (up to thirty-three **staves**) in use in England and Frisia (now Holland).

Armanen Runes: The eighteen-rune system synthesized by Guido von List in the 1900s.

Ásatrú: "True to the **Æsir**": the modern version of the heathen religion.

Asgard: The world of the gods at the top of the **World Tree**.

Athem: Breath of life.

Bind rune: A rune formed when two runes are joined.

Edda: Name for ancient manuscripts containing the mythological corpus of the North. The *Elder Edda* contains traditional mythic poems, and the *Younger Edda*, written c. 1222 C.E. by Snorri Sturluson was a handbook for **skalds**.

Elder: An experienced teacher of the folk.

Erulian: A **rune master**.

Etin: A giant, usually of great age and single-mindedness.

Fenris Wolf: One of the monsters **Loki** engendered. Will eventually become free and create **Ragnarök**.

Fetch: Personal warden, also a mental "image store."

Futhark: Abbreviated name for the runic alphabet, taken from the first row of runes.

Galdra: Verbal magic. Literal meaning: "to crow like a raven."

Galdrabók: Icelandic magical book from the 1500s. Contains much heathen material.

Hamingja: Personal power, luck.

Heathen: Originally meaning "country person" (heath), it came to mean a non-Christian person and now is a general term for anyone practicing the Germanic traditional religions.

Hel: Lowest world on the **World Tree**, the place of the dead.

Hugh: Intellectual/analytical parts of the mind/self.

Hyde: Body shape.

Initiation: Process of achieving a higher state of being, also the education in traditional lore.

Irminsûl: The sacred pillar representing the **World Tree**.

Jotunheim: Realm of the giants in the **Nine Worlds**.

Ljossalfheim: "Light Elf Home": a world in the **Nine Worlds**.

Loki: Trickster god of the **Æsir**. Troublesome, although sets in motion much of the mythic action.

Lyke: The body.

Mead: Traditional alcoholic drink made from honey. Could be made from wine or be alelike.

Midgard: "Middle Earth": the central world of the **Nine Worlds**.

Mjöllnir: **Thor's** magical hammer.

Muspellheim: The world of Cosmic Fire in the **Nine Worlds**.

Myne: Faculty of memory, reflectiveness aspect of the mind/self.

Niflheim: Realm of Cosmic Ice in the **Nine Worlds**.

Nine Worlds: The Northern mythic worlds that are connected via the roots of the **World Tree**. The universe of the runic tradition.

Norns: The three female "weavers of destiny" in the Germanic tradition.

Odian path: Emulating instead of worshipping Odin.

Odin: God of runes, magic, the dead, communication, and sovereignty.

OERP: *Old English Rune Poem.*

OIRP: *Old Icelandic Rune Poem.*

ONRP: *Old Norwegian Rune Poem.*

Ragnarök: Process of destruction and rebirth of the **Nine Worlds**, marked by the war of the gods and giants.

Rune: A character of the Germanic symbol system, also the mystery symbolized by the physical character.

Rune Gild: Group dedicated to the runes and their patron, **Odin**.

Rune master: Extremely experienced rune initiate dedicated to teaching runes; highly skilled at rune work.

Rune stave: The physical sign of the rune, also a rune carved on prepared wood.

Seidhr: Germanic type of shamanism and prophecy.

Shade: Soul.

Skald: Poet.

Skuld: One of the **Norns**; "that which shall be": the shaping of the future in rune divination.

Sleipnir: The mighty eight-legged horse of **Odin**.

Sumble: Sacred drinking ritual.

Sun wheel: Holy sign representing the sun.

Svartalfheim: "Dark Elf Home": the world of the dwarves (dark elves) in the **Nine Worlds**.

Thor: God of force, protection.

Troth: Loyalty (especially to gods, clan, self).

True: Loyal to the Northern gods and goddesses.

Tyr: God of justice, self-sacrifice.

Urdhr: One of the **Norns**, whose name means "that which has become."

Valhalla: The hall of the slain, dedicated to **Odin**.

Valknut: Knot of the Chosen, a ninefold angular design that symbolizes the **Odian path**.

Valkyrie: "Chooser of the Slain": female spirits who usher fallen warriors to **Asgard**.

Vanaheim: Home of the **Vanir** in the **Nine Worlds**.

Vanatru: "True to the **Vanir**": modern name for those who seek the path of the **Vanir**, also Germanic witchcraft.

Vanir: The gods of fertility and natural processes.

Verdhandi: One of the **Norns**, whose name means "that which is becoming."

Wode: Faculty of inspiration.

World Tree: Named **Yggdrasill**, the cosmic tree in the center of the universe, whose roots unite the **Nine Worlds**.

Wyrd: The web of synchronicity and cause and effect that the **Norns** govern.

Yggdrasill: The **World Tree**. Name means "Ygg's (Odin's) Horse."

Younger Futhark: The later sixteen rune rows used in Europe from c. 800 C.E. to 1100 C.E.

INDEX

QUICK REFERENCE

FEHU,
pp. 54–57
Energy, wealth,
new beginnings

URUZ,
pp. 58–61
Strength, vitality,
transformation

THURISAZ,
pp. 62–65
Will, reactive
force, Thor

ANSUZ,
pp. 66–69
Mind, self, Odin,
communication

RAIDHO,
pp. 70–73
Riding, pathway,
reason

KENAZ,
pp. 74–77
Creativity,
shaping, art

GEBO,
pp. 78–81
Gift, sacrifice,
hospitality

WUNJO,
pp. 82–85
Joy, harmony,
well-being

HAGALAZ,
pp. 86–89
Crisis, stress,
storm

NAUTHIZ,
pp. 90–93
Need, test,
ordeal

ISA,
pp. 94–97
Contraction,
stillness, silence

JERA,
pp. 98–101
Good harvest,
fruit, feast, cycles

IHWAZ,
pp. 102–105
The World Tree,
life and death

PERTHRO,
pp. 106–109
Chance,
synchronicity

ELHAZ,
pp. 110–113
Communication,
danger

SOWILO,
pp. 114–117
Goal, good
counsel, success

TIWAZ,
pp. 118–121
Victory, truth,
balance

BERKANO,
pp. 122–125
Liberation, release,
rebirth

EHWAZ,
pp. 126–129
Teamwork,
friendship, trust

MANNAZ,
pp. 130–133
Awareness,
awakening,
potential

LAGUZ,
pp. 134–137
Life force,
healing,
quickening

INGWAZ,
pp. 138–141
Hiding, separation,
gestation

DAGAZ,
pp. 142–145
Paradox,
synthesis,
consciousness

OTHALA,
pp. 146–149
Ancestral home,
well-being